Marriage is
for Losers

*A foolproof guide designed to help, hope and heal
Marital relationships*

A dvantage
BOOKS

By

Dr. John R. Adolph

This Guide Belongs To:

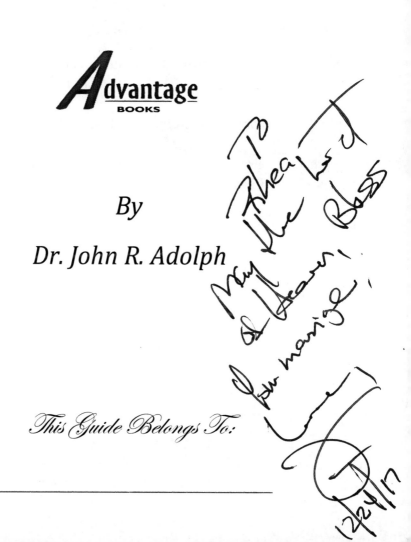

_____

Marriage is for Losers / Celibacy is for Fools by Dr. John R. Adolph
Copyright © 2016 by Dr. John R. Adolph
All Rights Reserved.
ISBN: 978-1-59755-410-7

Published by: ADVANTAGE BOOKS™
www.advbookstore.com

Unless otherwise indicated, all scripture quotations are taken from the Holy Bible King James Version (KJV). Public domain.

Library of Congress Control Number: 2016911233

This book is also available as an eBook everywhere eBooks are sold.
ISBN:978-1-59755-415-2

First Printing: August 2016
08 09 10 11 12 13 1410 9 8 7 6 5 4 3 2 1
Printed in the United States of America

DEDICATION

This work is dedicated to the finished work of my personal Lord and Savior Jesus Christ on the cross at Calvary. His love for his bride, the church, has been the core influence of this book.

To Mollyn Cole for writing the short stories used at the onset of each chapter of this book. You are so awesome!

To my loving, wonderful, beautiful wife, Dorrie (Baby), for her 16 years of love, care, friendship, commitment, patience, toil, support and prayers.

To my mother and father, Rev. Seymour V. and Barbara J. Adolph, for their life-long example of marital commitment.

To my mother-in-law and father-in-law, Pastor Vincent and First Lady Albertina Washington of Gardena, California who perpetually model marriage for our entire family to embrace.

To my siblings and their families, Pastor Seymour V. Adolph, Jr. (Jenny), Daisy Adrienelle English (Curtis), Ron L. Adolph (Wandy), my nieces, nephew, and relatives that have always been an ever present support system of love all of my life.

To the Married Couples Ministry of Antioch Missionary Baptist Church of Beaumont, Texas for their relentless pursuit in training, molding, shaping and strengthening marriages each week through the Word of God at the church.

To every engaged couple on the brink of marriage that are making plans to start a life together as one in the near future.

To every holy couple that has found marital happiness in honoring God in their marriage.

To every struggling couple that is on the verge of collapse, ruin and divorce.

To every married couple around the world that shares with me the glorious model of Christ and the Church through the covenant of marital commitment to be witnessed first by our families and friends and ultimately to be viewed by the world that we live in.

TABLE OF CIONTENTS

FOREWORD

I've been in the marriage business for fifty-five years. My wife Alyce and I married each other on December 1, 1956. Hundreds of couples have walked through the doors of my office, and expressed the joys and sorrows of married life. Few things in life have as much potential for bringing us happiness and unhappiness as do marital relationships.

In recent years, I've had a growing awareness that many couples today getting married have no clue of what makes a healthy marriage. So many people come from dysfunctional families where they have experienced so much hurt and pain, and they don't have a clear picture of a healthy family.

To say that marriage in Western culture is in trouble is an understatement. It is more accurate to say that married life has lost its way.

Dr. John R. Adolph challenges us in this book that marriage is for losers. Every couple must lose in order to win in your marriages. The fundamental building block in any relationship starts with God at the center. Only God can help us lose selfishness, lose an unforgiving spirit, lose the bad negative attitudes that we carry as baggage. Only God can keep us from arguments, and teach us to communicate by speaking and listening. Since none of us are perfect, nor always kind, thoughtful, understanding, considerate and loving, we need to learn how to forgive.

Dr. John R. Adolph nails it for us showing us how to do marriage God's way. I wished someone had pointed these principles out for me and my wife when we first started on our journey, the travel would have been much smoother.

I recommend Dr. John R. Adolph's book as a Christian guide for all married couples. What a blessing!

Thank God for it.

Samuel J. Gilbert Sr., D.Min
H.M.B.M.C., President

No one can argue the point that the complexion of marriage in the last 50 years has changed. Even since 1973 when my spouse and I were married, the words, "till death do us part" has a different meaning for the X-generation. Therefore, marriage for some is more of a rarity than the norm.

While visiting with Pastor Adolph and family during spring of 2009, the discussion of marriage took place. Pastor Adolph discussed with clarity, excitement and sincerity the stages of marriage, as he envisioned, for 21st century couples. These five stages as described by him; *your wine, no wine, need wine, get wine and good wine,* are the ideas that are found in John 2:1-12, as you will see discussed in this book.

Dr. Adolph has created a superb work in presenting the concept that when persons are looking to marry or for persons who have been married for one year, ten years or 25 years, marriage is an eternal testimony of God's miracle working power in the union. It is constant work!

My spouse and I have been married for 36 years come December. We have had from "wine" to "good wine". Serious illnesses, raising children, seen both children combat illnesses, graduate and post graduate study, care taking of parents, death of a parent, making financial ends meet, and moving toward retirement, etc. Just as Jesus performed the miracle at Cana in Galilee, He continues to do the same for us and will do the same for couples who approach the union of marriage and work to remain in marriage. It is the miracle that blesses helps, heals, strengthens and keeps couples together through the peeks, valleys, ups, downs, highs and lows of marriage.

Pastor Adolph and his beautiful wife Dorrie, weekly exemplify to thousands that staying married is possible. In this book, Dr. Adolph gives real life examples of how couples can "move through" and always be on the side of "good wine".

Thanks be to God the giver and John Adolph the crafter for this must read text on how miracles can happen in marriage.

Dr. Cleopatrick and Portia H. Lacy
Pastor and First Lady, Mount Zion Baptist Church – Griffin, GA

Note: Dr. Lacy was Pastor Adolph's Homiletics Professor at the Interdenominational Theological Center – Atlanta, GA.

PREFACE

It was a day that I will never forget as long as live. November 18, 1995, 1:00p.m. at Hopewell Baptist Church, Norcross, Georgia, Dr. William L. Sheilds Senior Pastor. It was my wedding day! It had been long anticipated and to be honest about it a day that I thought might not ever happen for a guy like me. Okay, let me be open and real with you as we share in literary fashion together. I was single for so long I thought that I would never find a wife. After I really dedicated my life to God I remained celibate for three years and eight months before marriage. I only slept with stuffed animals and I started naming them as I was without a life-long companion to share my time with. My relatives would always tell me that I was too picky, but I knew what I wanted and Dorrie Eileen was it.

My wedding day was like a dream that came true. My bride was gorgeous, my mother and father (now deceased) were both present, my family was there, my wife's family had traveled from the west coast to share this special day with us, my friends were in the house cheering me on, my pictures should have been placed in Jet Magazine (just my humble opinion of course), the reception was a party to remember, we honeymooned in Mexico, and returned to start the dream of "happily ever after together." But, what started off like a dream come true was quickly becoming a nightmare. My marriage became a headache so severe that Novocain could not remove the pain.

Within the short span of six months good communication became bad communication, sweet breath became morning breath, doors that once closed softly now started to slam shut, quality time became spare time, passion in the raw became pity with a rub, each day bore the similitude of hurricane season for those that live near the Gulf Coast (you never know when a storm is coming ashore), bills that were once paid were now bills that were either late or seriously delayed, cute habits quickly gained the annoying resemblance of a gnat at a summer picnic, my heartthrob was now causing me heartburn and I know that I was getting on her last nerve, but she was fresh out of those and I had worn out my welcome.

It's now Easter Sunday morning 1996 and we are headed to church for worship. Certainly one would think that good Christians could at least behave on Easter Sunday morning, but, not in the Adolph household that day. We argued like two drunken sailors in a saloon. To make matters even worse, I am preaching for a church as an interviewing candidate for the position of Senior Pastor. We step out of the truck onto the church parking lot as the "Good Rev. Doctor and his wife" that are seeking to lead the flock, so we stop the name calling and the heated debate. Worship was great but as soon as we get back into the truck we pick up where we left off. I no longer wanted to hear what she had to say to me so I turned my radio volume up as if to ignore her and she punched my radio silent (literally). The volcano of relational variance was erupting and hot lava was spilling out of my truck onto I-85 because things were way too hot for us to handle.

We get back to our apartment and I am completely affirmed that divorce is what's best for us. A few days later I fly to Houston to preach my father's spring revival and I am trying to find a way to break the news to my mom and dad that my marriage is over. I knew that I could not confront them with my domestic failure abruptly, so like Alex Rodriguez trying to steal second base, I slid into the conversation while they are eating dinner. I ask my mother, in the presence of my father, why she didn't end her marriage to him when he was a stoned alcoholic and the lights were turned off due to his uncontrollable addiction. I ask her why she didn't leave when there were rats in the house big enough to shoot with a pellet gun and roaches were everywhere. My mother lifted her head from her senior citizens plate at IHOP located off of Normandy in Houston, Texas off of the East Freeway and she said, "Bobby, when I married your daddy it was for better or for worst. Those were some tough times, but the Lord helped us get through them. Things are so much better now for all of us. We sacrificed for the good of this family. My children are all grown and degreed, all of my houses are paid for including that one, I have a new Cadillac sitting outside and a Lincoln Town Car sitting on my driveway. God kept us together as a family. And besides all of that, if I didn't divorce you with all of the hell you put me through growing up I surely wasn't leaving your daddy. You turned out alright and so did he. Now hand me some napkins and find me some ketchup." My father's chest poked out like he was a body builder on stage showing the world his pecks and I felt like a mosquito trying to swallow a watermelon.

When I returned home to Atlanta I began to seek God like never before about my marriage and how to make things work. With the wisdom of my parents in my spirit and the Word of the Lord in my soul I discovered the secret that can keep a couple married until death separates one of them from the other. I have the remedy that will keep divorce from haunting hurting couples. God has given me the relational resolve that will keep the demon of divorce away. I have been blessed to have in my heart the vitamins that will strengthen weak couples and make strong couples even stronger. And, I am absolutely for certain that the Lord has blessed me with an antidote for marital misery that will restore any weak marriage and cause it to be stronger than it has ever been. That secret will serve as the core, centre and crux of this work. It is simple. It is profound. It is foolproof. It never fails and it works every time. Here it is at the onset of this book, download this concept onto the frontal lobe of your intellect and keep it as you share each chapter with me, "Marriage Is For Losers!"

INTRODUCTION

Marriage requires a complete sacrifice from both parties involved. However, the word sacrifice means almost nothing to the generation that we now live in. In a culture where we Facebook, Tweet, Google, email, text message, Skype, swipe, and win at all cost the term sacrifice just has no place in our vocabulary. I mean, we have heard of a sacrifice fly in baseball or we may have even heard of a sacrifice bunt when you're trying to help the runner on first get to second base. But, the term sacrifice in our culture has almost died. But, there is another term that we can use in the place of sacrifice that all of us can relate to and that is the word "lose".

We don't like losers at all. We hate losing. In fact, if a team is a winner we will buy their jersey at full cost and say "we won!" But, if that same team loses we will drop that jersey (unless you're just a diehard fan) and say "they lost." Losers never get the trophy. The articles written about losers are always depressing. The attitude of a loser is always filled with a melancholy mood and losers never get the prize in the end. But, here's some wonderful news for every engaged and married couple reading this book right now, we lose to win!

By now you have to know that I am a faithful believer in the Lord Jesus Christ. If you have not figured that out just yet, let me just tell you straight out, I love the Lord with all of my heart. And, real Christians live in what I call the ever-present paradox of victory. By this I mean, our victories are always best seen in what appears to be our losses. Jesus Christ is our divine model of this reality. He lost it all including his life. Yet on the back of His loss has come our greatest win. We have it all because He lost it all! Jesus became a loser for us to become winners. And, if we want to see marriages last, families gain strength, and relationships stand the test of time we must copy the Lord's example of losing in marriage for family to win, for just like His cross required someone to lose for others to win, marriage requires a loser too. When you decide to lose, you will win, your spouse will win, your family will win and the Kingdom of our God will celebrate victory for the cause of faith! But, it will only come to mature believers that are bold enough in belief to live out the reality that says to the world "Marriage is for Losers!"

This book is designed to impact couples by sharing very important relational ideals that must be sacrificed if marriage is to thrive. In short, this work is going to tell you what you have to lose for your marriage to win. Each chapter begins with a story that is called "Winners that are Losing." The names, if any, used in each narrative have been changed to protect the true identity of those actually involved. Read the narrative with an open mind and see if you can relate to what is happening to the couple being discussed. Trust me, if you can't identify with them now there may certainly come a day or even a season in your marriage when you will able to relate to them. After the opening story there will be a segment in each chapter called "Lessons on Losing for those that want to Win." This is where practical principles will be presented for the purpose of helping a couple fully understand what must be lost in order for their family to actually see the gain.

The next section of each chapter is called the "Losers Bracket" in which both persons in the relationship have to answer some critical questions about themselves and their marital relationship. Please be open and honest in this segment. Your honesty in this section will prove to be your healing balm for sections that are yet to come. And finally the chapter concludes by having each person perform a faith function. This concluding segment is called the "Winners Circle." Take the exercise within this section of the chapter seriously and perform it with great passion. You may not want to do it. But, those who dare to do it in faith will find themselves losing only to discover that when you learn to lose your marriage will ultimately win.

CHAPTER 1

LOSE DIVORCE AS AN OPTION

The Story: Winners That Are Losing

Nag, nag, nag! Wash the car, clean the garage, mow the lawn, trim the hedges, put your shoes away, hang up your suits, find the remote, close the door, open the door, pick up the dry cleaning, go to the store, kill the mosquitoes, spray the flies, feed the dog, investigate things that go bump in the night, sit through chick-flicks, put it down, pick it up – gosh! When did I sign up for all of this? I should have known it was going to be a mistake to marry someone so stubborn and strong-willed. At least when I was single I was my own boss. All of those same things still had to be done, but I was the captain of my own ship which meant that I could do them when I wanted to --- if I wanted to. Now, I go to work every day, make the money, bring *some* of it home, then start the extreme 'honey-do' cycle all over again every single day in my house. I'm the king of this castle and I'm being treated like a servant by the queen. None of this was listed in the job requirements section of our marriage vows. I want a divorce.

Nag, nag, nag! Wake him up, put him to sleep, gas up the car, sweep the garage, tell him what to do, pick up after him, hide the *!#% remote, pay bills, drop off the dry cleaning, cook three squares a day, keep extra everything on hand for the boys on any given game day, clean the house, keep every TV in the house tuned to the sports channel, take care of *his* kids, pacify *their* mamas, put up with baby-mama-drama, take care of *his* mama --- gosh! When did I sign up for all of this? I should have known it was going to be a mistake to marry someone that had baggage but no dolly. At least when I was single I was my own boss. All of those same things still had to be done, but I was the only 'Diva on Deck' which meant that I could do them when I wanted to --- if I wanted to. Now, I go to work every day, make the money, bring *most* of it home, then start my chores all over again every single day in my house. I'm supposed to be the queen of this castle instead I feel like a chambermaid; a housekeeper; a servant.

None of this was listed in the job requirements section of our marriage vows. I want a divorce!

I mean, what does she want from me? Maybe I need to trade her in for a younger model; a fresher model; one whose sole purpose is to care for me. I look at other married couples and it doesn't seem like they have the problems we have. They are cruising, dancing, and traveling. I want to do some of that. Why is there a problem if I want to have the guys over to watch the game in my house? Why do we have to discuss purchasing a hot rod or a Harley? I work hard every day and have the right to do as I please in my house. She is my wife, not my mother; I don't have to clear anything with her. The more I think about it the more convinced I am that I should send her packing. I can get a new life and a new wife all in one fell swoop and still be able to enjoy it all if I cancel her contract now; divorce her now.....

He must think I am crazy. What happened to all of that red carpet treatment that he rolled out when he was courting me? Why do I pay a nail technician to massage my feet then haggle with him over the nickels and dimes it cost me to get it done? I work hard every day and should not have to justify every cent of my expenditures to him. But even if I didn't work on someone else's job every day, all of the things I do for him are more than enough to warrant some niceties for myself. I don't need the aggravation. I feel like I would get treated better if I were somebody else's lady-in-waiting rather than his wife. As a matter of fact, I did get treated better as somebody else's lady-in-waiting. He is my husband, not my father; I don't have to clear my schedule with him. The more I think about it the more I am convinced that he should pack his stuff and go. Yeah, that's it; he should go. It's my house any doggone way. What does he look like barking orders at me in my house? Furthermore, what kind of idiot do I look like obeying them....in my house? He needs to learn that it costs to be the boss. If I divorce him I could be free to await the arrival of someone who walks tall and carries a big stick. Divorce sounds like the right move right about now...

<u>Lessons On Losing For Those That Want To Win</u>

This may sound completely crazy, but it's true when you really think about it. We never think of divorcing anyone except for the person that we are married to. We have family members that are as crazy as lunatics that live in the padded walls of an asylum, but we don't divorce them. We have friends that we know need professional help from time to time, and we stick with them. But, when our spouses miss the mark too many times we are ready to call in the attorney and find some way to get them out of our lives so that we can move on without them. In fact, some people get married with thoughts of divorce on their minds before the wedding day is over.

I once did a wedding at a huge chapel for a couple. The décor was gorgeous, the wedding party was stunning, and the flowers were breath taking. The groom stood there tall and handsome next to me as his bride came strolling down the aisle. I started the ceremony with a prayer and the reading of the scriptures. I then had the bride and groom face each other and join hands for the purpose of sharing their vows with each other. But, when I got to the section of the vows that said "…for better or for worse; for richer or for poorer…" the bride would not repeat it. I cleared my throat and repeated the section as if she were hard of hearing. The bride looked at me and said, "Reverend skip that part because I am getting married for better and for richer. If he cannot help me with those I am out of here and he knows it." The groom stood there grinning and nodding so I moved on. But it was clear to me and to the groom that divorce would be an option if he did not keep better and richer on the horizon of his life at all times.

Let's face it marriage has stages just like nature gives us seasons. When it is hot outside you don't give up on life and quit. You put on a really nice summer piece with some cute sandals and move on looking good and feeling great. When it is freezing outside you don't stop living. You find a turtle neck shirt, some long-johns, a heavy coat, a hat and scarf wrap-up and move forward. Likewise, marriage has seasons or stages within it. Don't leave your partner because the stage is uncomfortable. You adjust to the season and move forward with them.

The very first miracle that Jesus performed when He started His earthly ministry was not saving a man's soul or opening a blind man's eyes. His first miracle happened at a wedding. Why? He knew that it would take a miracle to keep a married couple together. According to St. John 2:1-11, marriage has five stages. Stage 1: your wine; stage 2: no wine; stage 3: need wine; stage 4: get wine, and stage 5: new wine. Let's briefly examine each stage for a moment.

In stage one of marriage that I call "your wine" things are sweet. In this season of marriage your partner may not be perfect, but they are perfect for you. Love and romance are in the air. Their touch makes you happy; their presence can make an empty room full. And your commonalities flood you. But, please understand this one emphatic principle; this stage does not last forever. Like a cute little baby that becomes a toddler, your marriage grows past stage 1. Stage 1 does not die, it just fades away. And in struts stage 2 that I call "no wine." This is the stage of marriage when you both know that something is different. You're going through the motions of sipping the sweet wine that you used to have, but the goblets are empty and you know it. The touch isn't the same. The feeling isn't the same and you no longer celebrate the things that you share in common because the things that you have that contrasts are killing you. It is during this season of marriage that couples often try to make some new wine so they try taking a second honeymoon, rekindling the fire or increasing their time of touching, praying and dating. But when all is concluded the glass of sweet wine that once flooded your cup is now gone.

In sprints stage 3 which I call "need wine." During this stage of the relationship marriage can be a total misery. The person that once caused you joy has now become the centerfold of your sorrow and the relationship is a burden. Third party intrusions float in under the radar like spy aircraft loaded with destructive missiles that land in your living room. Going home after a long day of work can be like walking into path of an F-5 tornado with no shelter in sight. Unmet needs often lead to the demonic attack of extra-marital affairs, in-laws become outlaws, money woes become money wars, and things go from bad to worse and from worse to divorce-sounds-like-a-winner-to-me. It is during this stage of marriage that divorce is most likely to happen. But, I submit to you that if you quit in stage 3 you will miss the victory of stage 5.

In strolls stage 4 or what I call the "get wine" stage. This is the phase of marriage where the God of Heaven reminds us that the only way a marriage can make it is for Him to hold it together for you. In the narrative recorded in John 2, the people at the wedding run out of wine but, Jesus tells the servants to go and get water. Here's the problem, what Jesus just told these people to do made no sense at all. They have plenty of water, they need wine. But, in faith they did it and the end result was the sweetest wine they had ever tasted. The same thing happens to us that dare to obey the commands of God in the midst of living out the covenant that we have made with Him when we said "...for better or for worse..." If you want the sweet wine of your marriage to return someone has to be bold enough to do exactly what the Lord says do even if it doesn't make any sense to you. And when you walk by faith to do it, the God of Heaven moves because He is faithful and supplies your every need. This is an awesome phase of the relationship. It is here that you apologize for things that you didn't do wrong, love your spouse for what they did not do and for what they could have done but refused to do. Pride is erased, humility is increased; prayers are made; perseverance and determination are personified by belief, and love is present not because of what your spouse is, but in spite of what they are. It is here that losing starts to happen.

Finally in slides stage 5, or what I like to call "new wine." This is where the wine of marital bliss is sweet, but this time it is sweeter than it was the last time because it is love that comes from God, for God and never, ever runs out again. In fact, your "new wine" will fill you when "your old wine" is nowhere to be found. This is greatest stage of marriage because the "new wine" is sweeter than any wine that you've ever had in your lifetime. However, the only way for you to have the sweet wine of stage 5 is to lose divorce as an option.

For those of you that are old school, you know what it is like to play cards; Black Jack, Pitty Pat, Poker, and Uno. Spades was always my game. If you are a spadeologist like I am, then you know that if you plan to win you have to get the weak cards out of your hand as soon as the games starts if you intend to win. Like weak cards in the game of spades, divorce is weak. If you keep it in your hand it will cost you the game and your marriage will fail. But, if you throw divorce out of your hand from the very beginning you can never use it and it cannot hurt you because you don't have it to play anymore!

Lose divorce as an option and you will stay married forever!

The Losers Bracket

- What are some things that would make you say "this marriage is over?" Be open and honest.

- Have you ever threatened your spouse with divorce or thought about it? Why did you want out?

- What are some things that your spouse does that really get on your last nerve? Be specific.

- What are some habits that you have that you know are really ugly and need work? Be real.

- What stage of marriage are you in right now? How does it make you feel?

- If you keep divorce as an option in marriage one day you will use it. Are you willing to lose divorce as an option so that your marriage can last forever?

The Winners Circle

- Take a sheet of paper. Write at the top of your page this title "Good Reasons to Get A Divorce." Now openly, honestly, and candidly list every single reason you would consider a divorce, file for separation or even end your marriage. You may list any and everything that comes to mind. Young married and engaged couples often have a hard time thinking of reasons that they would want to end it. However, couples that have been married a few years may need more than one sheet paper. Add sheets if necessary, but do not write on the back side of the page. Please be honest about everything.

- Once your list is complete fold it so that none of your reasons for divorce are visible. Take a pen or pencil and draw a huge cross on the side of the page that has no writing on it. Now close your eyes and imagine a man that knows everyone of your faults, secret sins, mistakes and mess-up's. Picture Him being nailed to a tree alive. Now ask this man "why are you doing this?" And hear His voice say "I am willing to lose it all not to let you go!"

- Open your eyes and hold your list up before your face. The cross should be visible but your reasons for divorce should be hidden. This is how Jesus Christ see's you. His reasons to divorce you would fill twice the number of pages that you have just listed for your spouse. But the reason He refuses to leave you is because He loved you enough to lose so that you could win. If your marriage is going to live forever you must do the same.

Now pray this prayer, "Lord, if you have not given up on me, I cannot give up on you and leave the spouse that I am covenanted to. I have made you a promise and I plan to keep it. I believe in my heart and receive in my spirit that what you have joined together no man or circumstance can cause it to go under and become void. My marriage will last forever because divorce is not an option. We will make it and be happy knowing that our lifestyle of marriage makes you happy. In Jesus' name. Amen!"

Take the sheet(s) and rip it into as many pieces as you can. Nothing written on any sheet is worth a divorce.

CHAPTER 2

LOSE THE NOTION OF "HAPPILY EVER AFTER"

The Story: Winners That Are Losing

Wife: "Hello."

The ex-wife on speakerphone: Hey; let me speak to your husband….about our son. I know my son is always there with you because his father is always *wor-king*(yeah, right), but you don't count. You're just 'this one' on the way to the next one. Keep saying good morning; you'll see. As a matter of fact, never mind; I'll just go see him at work tomorrow and we will handle the matter in person --- together.

Wife: Apparently he had the right to remain silent, because he did. Mom and Dad always encouraged me to get an education, embrace and ensconce myself in a career that answered my calling, solidify professional upward mobility, procure residential stability, keep my female goods preserved and packaged nicely, get married, have 2.5 children, frame it all with a white picket fence, then ride off into the sunset as I lived happily ever after. Where can I buy that package? Two tickets please!

He and I were the "it" couple back in the day. Of course time and temptation drove us apart on more than one occasion, but this was supposed to be "it". We were older, wiser --- blah, blah, blah. Apparently, that doesn't mean a darn thing. It seemed that every time I turned around I was passively confronting more obstacles that I felt he should have been shielding me from. Wasn't that the man's job? Wasn't that the husband's job? I mean, we weren't just hanging out until we found something better to do. He asked me to marry him. He was the king of the castle and the head of the household yet I felt I was communing with the annoying paparazzi rather than rolling with the royals. Simply put, we were not prepared when the harsh realities of everyday life descended upon us with an intrusive and offensive thud. We suddenly found ourselves overcome by the tsunamic waves of external pressures which caused an immediate shift in our relational dynamic.

Where were the flowers? Even though they always made me sneeze, he insisted on sending them because they represented the time-honored art of traditional courtship. Where was the heart-shaped box of chocolates? Why did he stop surprising me with overnight trysts on the weekend? Why did he stop our shared candlelit baths? Why did he stop asking me to sing to him? Why did he stop randomly texting and calling me with sweet nothings throughout the course of the workday? Why is it all so routine now? So boring and so bland; so unfulfilling…

Husband: I feel like I am caught in the middle. On the one hand, my wife has astronomically high expectations and on the other hand, my ex-wife has me over a barrel. I am literally doomed either way it goes. My wife is supposed to understand the delicate balance needed to keep the peace so that I can grow a relationship with my son. She is supposed to understand that she and I both will have to take one for the team when it comes to dealing with my ex. It wasn't a problem before, but now it is. Why? Dealing with her disdain regarding issues and people connected to my son exasperates me and does more harm than good. But then she expects me to carry on as if nothing happened. I used to love to slip into the tub with her while she was preparing for bed. Now, all I want is a break from the tension. I don't want to go on weekend jaunts; I want to spend that time with my son. She and I are already married so I don't need to work on things with her. I need to work on developing a stronger relationship with him.

Everything has changed. I used love to listen to my wife sing. It didn't matter what genre of music she was singing, I just wanted to hear it; her. She always protested that she needed to improve, but I had never heard anything more beautiful. Now, I just want silence. No singing, no arguing, no talking, no nothing. Shut up!

Isn't this how things took a wrong turn in my first marriage? I don't understand how and why it is happening again. I thought things were going to be better the second time around. I expected some bumps in the road, but never this. I am so not happy and I hate being married…..

Lessons On Losing For Those That Want To Win

Hollywood has done a job on us that is going to take years of real teaching to reverse. People get married because they want to be happy. The real trouble is that most of these people were miserable living by themselves and then they think that they are going to take their misery, find the perfect person to marry and then mix their personal misery with the misery of another that will somehow result in marital happiness. It is crazy, ludicrous, ignorant and foolish to say the least.

I once sat with a young couple that spent over $70,000.00 on their wedding. They had enough calla-lilies in the cathedral to fill a green house nursery to capacity. Her wedding gown costs at least $20,000.00 and the after party was a smash! A full 20 piece orchestra, ice sculptures were everywhere, some of them with two love birds dripping water from their beaks. The menu was surf and turf, prime rib and lobster. When it was time for the toast they had imported wine from Africa to sip on. They cruised the Mediterranean and returned to a nice home in Kingwood Forest, a suburb of Houston, Texas. They just have to be happy right? Wrong. Eighteen months after they married they found themselves sitting in my office struggling because they both discovered that their marriage made them unhappy.

Please retain this one emphatic Christian principle, marriage is not for the happy it is a lifestyle for the holy. Holiness is what marriage presents to God and it makes Him happy. When you learn to make God happy with your lifestyle that is holy, then and only then, will you learn to be happy. Here's the problem, in most marriages we are not living to make God happy we are married asking God to make us happy while we are living and it is not happening. True marital happiness comes to the couple that has enough faith, trust and belief in the Lord to say to Him, "Lord if you loved me enough to die for me, I love you enough to live each day for you." This is how happiness happens.

In Ephesians 5:21-33 the Apostle Paul teaches the church at Ephesus how a husband and a wife can take a marriage and make it produce sweet melodies, wonderful harmonies, and fine music together. Like the conductor of the Chicago philharmonic orchestra, Paul lays out the score for each married man and woman that desires to see a real marriage make a plush and vivacious sound. I believe that within the confines of the above listed passage lies the real secret of marital holiness, that if practiced will please God and produce a happiness that is enjoyed by mature believers and often longed for by couples that are married and miserable. Let's briefly explore the passage together for a moment.

One of the biggest secrets in marriage that helps make it holy is mutual submission. That's right. Not just the woman is to submit to the man, but they both must submit to God whole-heartedly. Mutual submission suggests that the relationship will be done for God and not for the persons in the covenant. I often ask young couples "why are you getting married?" And I often hear all types of nice reasons that are big on aroma but short on flavor. I've heard "I want to get married so that I won't have to be lonely." I have heard this one too, "I wanted to have sex so I am tying the knot." And, of course I have heard this one time and time again, "I have always dreamed of having a beautiful wedding." None of these answers are the root cause as to why a believer should even ponder getting married. Here's the right answer, "I want to get married because I want to live a completely submitted lifestyle that pleases God by loving another in a covenant as He loves me." Mutual submission suggests that this is being done for the glory and honor of God and it will be done His way or no way at all. When this is done by both parties involved the marriage strikes a major chord and beautiful marital music begins.

Once the music starts, a melody can only be heard if the next secret is in place. The right roles and responsibilities must be practiced. In other words, a woman must submit herself to her husband just like she would submit herself to her God. And, the man, who is already submitted to God, must love his bride like Jesus loves the church. I once went to a picnic with a group of men from the church. The wives of the older men were fixing their husbands plates and making sure that their beverages stayed cold and pampering them. The young men all had to fix their own food. Not one young wife moved a muscle. When we got back to the table, one of the young men said "now that's how you should train a woman to treat a man." But, an old bald headed man put him in his place and responded, "that's not training, that's years of love! If you love her she will submit to you. But, if you try training her all hell will break loose." Love is the melody of marriage that keeps the music of the relationship sweet enough to charm your soul.

The great crescendo of any marital masterpiece happens when we realize that marriage is not about the two people within it, but about the God that governs it. In verse 32 of Ephesians 5 Paul lets the reader know that when he speaks of a man and a woman in marriage the real hidden mystery within it is that he is actually speaking about Christ and His church. This is such an awesome idea and reality. When God wants people to see what He looks like loving His bride, He shows people you and your spouse. Imagine for a moment that you were God. Okay, I know that's a huge stretch, but just pretend. Now imagine being married to someone like you. How long would you last honestly? Yet the Lord has patiently remained faithful to you and there have been numerous times that He has not been happy with you at all. But, He didn't leave you. Why? God knows that the covenant that we share has nothing to do with happiness, but everything to do with holiness.

Just as the Lord has remained with us in spite of our flaws, failures, and foolishness He wants us to have the same resolve with our spouses. Now this is a marriage that is making sweet, sweet music!

The Losers Bracket

- Who are you really living for? Are you living to please God? Or, are you living simply to make yourself happy?

- Which is most important to you being happy or being holy?

- Jesus Christ lost it all just to make you holy. How much are you willing to lose for Him to make Him happy?

- Marriage was designed to make sweet music. If we could listen to the music of your marriage right now what would it sound like? Be honest.

- Have you resolved to do marriage God's way as it relates to mutual submission?

- In total honesty what are some things that just make you unhappy with your spouse?

- What are some things that make you unhappy with yourself?

Welcome To The Winners Circle

Pray this petition to God:

Lord, there are times that I am unhappy in my marriage. It hurts me deeply and causes me discomfort, disgust and sometimes depression. But, I know that there are times I cause you unhappiness. When I sin knowing that it is not the right thing to do or even the right thought to think you remain with me in spite of not being happy with me. God if you can do this for me, I can do the same for my spouse. Help me Lord learn to live simply to make you happy. Cause me to walk in such a way that the joy of my life is to bring a smile upon your face. And please God, I beg you, help me to stop examining the things that make me unhappy in my marriage and make me to examine what makes me unhappy in my heart. Cleanse me O Lord of the desire to gratify myself through my spouse and help me to glorify you through my marital covenant. I thank you right now for a holy marriage that you can be happy with. In the name of Jesus Christ I pray. Amen.

CHAPTER 3

LOSE THE ARGUMENT

The Story: Winners That Are Losing

Sharon to Michael, Sr.: Can't you get a better job? You need to get a better job. You need to make more money. What kind of man can't provide for his family? I want to go shopping somewhere other than the same place where I buy our groceries. I want to go on trips, and I want to go to the casino. Why can't I do any of that? How come the kids are still wearing the same school clothes they wore at the beginning of the year? Why didn't you get a Christmas bonus? We barely had any toys under the tree for the kids this year. Did you see how disappointed they were when they woke up and saw that Santa had 'gypped' them? You knew this Christmas was coming since last Christmas; why didn't you make it happen for our kids? You go to work every single day and this is all we have to show for it? Kids, thank your dad.

Michael, Jr. and Stacy: Thanks, dad.

Sharon to Michael, Sr: Some MAN of the house you are… and why are we still living in this raggedy house anyway? Why don't you give it to one of your other siblings? Better yet, sell it to one of your siblings and build me the home you promised me. You're the only one attached to this shack since you grew up here, but we need something much bigger and much better than this. I guess your mama called herself leaving this as part of her legacy for you and the kids, but I don't want any part of this. I need some central air and heat and not some antiquated window units. I need to tear down some walls so I can have an open floor plan. I need some columns, arches, fireplaces, tilework, hardwood, granite, stainless steel, skylights --- where is all of that? How are you going to give me that if you can't do nothing more than put some little choo-choo trains under the tree? Kids, thank your dad.

Michael, Jr. and Stacy: Thanks, dad.

Sharon to Michael, Sr: And it smells in here. Is that mold? You have us living in this dusty, moldy house enough to kill us all. I wish a hurricane would blow through here and level this piece of trash. At least that way we can start over and build something decent from the ground up. That would be the best thing to happen to this house --- that is, IF you paid the insurance premiums. Have you paid the insurance premium? Is it current? Is that why we've been going without --- so you could cover the premiums? Probably not. You never do anything right. We'll probably have to wade through tons of governmental red tape to get some kind of public assistance to replace the house. Now what? The space heater is out yet again. It's 30 degrees outside in the middle of January! Let me guess: your masterplan is to freeze me and the kids to death so you can collect the life insurance money and start over with some young little floozy, right? I think not. You are such a wonderful man and a great provider; you are truly a catch. Kids, thank your dad.

Michael, Jr. and Stacy: Thanks, dad.

Sharon to Michael, Sr: And is it too much to ask for a car that was built in this century? I mean --------------------------- !!!**&!@#$%&&!!

Michael Jr: Hello, 911? I think you should come. My mom was talking and my dad wasn't. Now Dad is choking Mom. She is on the floor and he is on top of her. He told us to go to our room. We did, but he is still on top of her with his hands around her neck. She says she can't breathe. You should probably come.

The police arrived within minutes from their nearby substation to find Michael, Sr. being restrained by an equally strong male neighbor, while paramedics were attending to the bruises on Sharon's neck. Sharon exclaimed, "I don't know what happened to Michael. He just snapped. We've been married fifteen years and this has never happened before. I think he's stressed out on the job and with his siblings" upon seeing the police arrive. She further added "Ya'll need to take him for a cooling-off period because this doesn't make any sense. I spend all my time taking care of him and making sure he is happy and healthy and this is the thanks I get? Oh, no. Is this how you're supposed to treat a loving wife? No!"

The police began searching for Michael, Sr. when they finally arrived at the end of Sharon's sworn statement of innocence and bewilderment. They feared that he had fled to avoid prosecution. After canvassing the neighborhood, they were surprised to find that Michael, Sr. was sitting in the rear of the squad car. The in-car-cam showed him calmly walking over to the car, opening the door, and sitting down in the backseat, without guidance or restraints. There he sat...........peacefully.

Lessons On Losing For Those That Want To Win

I was shocked to discover that the vast majority of police calls that happen after the sun down in the small metropolis of Beaumont, Texas where I live all have to do with domestic violence. I spoke to one of my very dear friends that works for the police force and he informed me that it is worse than what he could ever dare report. Husbands are beating wives like Muhammed Ali beat George Foreman in his heavyweight title bout in the Rumble in the Jungle where he discovered the rope-a-dope. And, wives are scratching up husbands like a cat of the back of a German Shepherd that has just found out that size does not always matter. Domestic violence is happening and it must come to a halt!

The root cause of many of these disputes stem from communication that has become heated and things simply get out of control. Okay, let's be real honest for a moment. No one can get on your nerves like your spouse can. And, it feels good to win a heated debate, especially when you know that you're right. But, when all is finished, what do you win if your spouse has hurt feelings, damaged emotions and things go from verbal sparring to physically fighting? Here's the real answer, you accomplish nothing at all. Truthfully speaking, you have done more harm than you will ever do good. If you want the horrible communication of argumentative debate to stop between you and your spouse simply decide to lose the argument and let them win the verbal sparring match.

Abuse whether physical or verbal can be very damaging. But, verbal abuse does more damage in the long run. It can cause depression, codependency, hypertension and other stress related illnesses that are life threatening. However, in the wisdom filled book of Proverbs there is a verse filled with compassion that can heal moments of combative communication. It says, *"A soft answer turns away wrath, but grievous words stir up anger" (Proverbs 15:1a).* In other words, if you speak kindly to each other things will not get heated and out of control, but if you yell and scream things are going to become heated and boil over on the stove of your relationship and anger is going to become your new reality. Remember this huge Christian principle; words are like bullets in a gun. Once you shoot them they are gone and the damage has been done.

The only way to have a good argument is for two out-of-control people to open their big mouths and let each other have it verbally. The best way to avoid an argument is to learn the art of keeping your mouth shut, walking away if need be and being mature enough in the faith to love your spouse in moments when they are not lovable. Arguments can only happen if two people participate. If you want the argument to end keep your mouth shut and use your tongue to heal your spouse and not hurt them at all.

Large buildings have fire safety evacuation plans in place to protect people just in case a fire occurs. Like a large building with a fire safety plan, the best time to protect your relationship against an argument is before it ever takes place. Every married couple should have an evacuation plan in place that both parties agree to before any form of heated debate ever takes place. One couple that I counseled some years ago had a very creative safety plan that they used to protect themselves from any heated conversation. Their plan was simple. If their voices got above a normal tone one of them would call time out and they would not discuss that issue or any related matter for thirty six hours (3 days). When the time out period was over they could resume the conversation. Believe it or not, the time that they spent in agreed upon silence gave them time to pray, mediate, and contemplate the best possible way to talk to each other without yelling and arguing.

I was raised and reared by older people that gave me godly wisdom and it holds true, especially for those that are involved in the covenanted relationship of marriage. It simply says "if you don't have anything kind to say don't say anything at all."

If you never want to have ill words spoken between you and the one that you loved enough to marry, lose the argument and move on.

The Losers Bracket

• Your spouse can get on your last nerve from time to time. What are some things that they do that just make you seemingly have to say something negative to them?

• How often do you and your spouse get into heated conversations and arguments?

• What seems to be the root cause of the debates?

• What can you do differently to avoid heated debates in your marriage?

• Are you willing to use kind words to heal your spouse and bless them in conversation? If so, what kind words can you use that would bless them today? Be specific.

The Winners Circle

There are two assignments attached to this chapter. First, write your spouse a note or buy them a card. Share with them your desire never to argue with them again as long as you are married to them. If you have had some really serious arguments in the past apologize for your role in each of them. This is not an admission of any right or wrong. But, if you were wrong or could have done things differently admit it. At the conclusion of the letter invite your spouse to set up a time to meet with you for at least an hour. Once the meeting time and date has been set I want you engage each other in assignment two. I want you design, develop and agree upon an evacuation plan to be put in to place that will keep you from hurting each other in heated arguments for the remainder of your life together. The plan does not have to be complex, but it does need to exist and be understood and agreed upon by each of you.

CHAPTER 4

LOSE THE UNFORGIVENESS

The Story: Winners that are Losing

Things were going along rather well at the class reunion. We were looking sharp and feeling fine when a blast from the past bowled me over as if bowling were an Olympic sport. There he was, shaking hands with others as he went from table to table getting reacquainted with old friends. I had forgotten all about him and our dalliance until I saw my husband eyeing his date. Then it all came flooding back like a recurring nightmare. My husband had a roving eye and wandering hands when we were dating. One of our pre-marital splits occurred when I discovered that he had slept with his friend's girlfriend. I know that anything goes with some men, but he and this gentleman were closer than close. They shot marbles and skipped rocks together as children. Not only was it hurtful to me, it ruined their friendship. Our relationship was a casualty of their tryst, but the story did not end there. I had known for many years prior that his friend was interested in me. My husband had told me about his friend's interest in me at the very beginning of our relationship. He wasn't my type and I was already madly in love with him, so there was nothing to fear. However, he started looking really good to me after the revelation of our significant others' betrayal.

I slipped him my card one evening after an innocent social gathering at the Swing Out hotspot. He had held me quite closely while we danced, and I found myself not being bothered by the fact that he was not my type. I was more interested in retribution; vindication, payback. We would converse for hours on end and occasionally met for dinner and a movie. Things were progressing nicely until our closeness was discovered by our cheating significant others. His ex was quietly ranting, but mine was having a full-blown fit. I guess there is just something about the male ego that allows them to dish it out but they can't take it to save themselves! My ex (now husband) miraculously showed up at the local hotspot in the hopes of intimidating him. Being young and foolish, I milked it for all it was worth. I painted a picture that said we were far closer than we actually were. So what? He had actually slept with her! The last thing he saw was us leaving the hotspot – together.

Now, here we are years later. We've reconciled, and so have they. Seeing my husband eyeing her and doing all he could to position himself to engage her truly enraged me. The one time we did discuss those events, my mouth spoke forgiveness but clearly my heart is saying something different tonight. I still can't believe I did it, but while my hubby was planning a covert-op, I boldly walked right up to Mr. tall, dark, and very handsome, warmly embraced him, and led him to the dance floor. My husband was so stunned that he literally froze in his tracks. He stood there and watched this muscle-bound gentleman hold me close. I wanted him to watch. He needed to watch. He needed to know how much it hurt each time his cheating ways were rubbed in my face.

When the song ended my husband was suddenly ready to leave. He looked furious and broken. I felt triumphant. I knew this was not the way to handle things in a marriage, but I had endured so much. She was not his first indiscretion… . I wanted him to feel what I felt *each time* he had strayed.

Silence. All the way home there was nothing but deafening silence. No music, no conversation, no nothing. I began happily humming along to add further insult to injury. He finally pulled over and chastised me for what I did. I fought back with the truth; he was ticked because this time I did it to him before he did it to me. I showed him a cell phone video of him staring at her and methodically attempting to stage things so he could steal some moments with her. I beat him at his game, in his face, and in front of his friends.

So much time had elapsed since that chapter in our lives that I had forgotten all about it until that night. I probably would not have reacted as such had he not begun acting like a private investigator and stalking this woman. While he was busy trying to sneak around, I simply walked straight up to him and got what I wanted. The truth is, my husband's guilt has convicted me. His friend and I never did anything inappropriate. We did not sleep together. We had far too much respect for ourselves and each other to indulge as such. Still, we allowed them to think otherwise. The night we left together was beautiful; he walked me to my car, followed me home, and waited until I got in safely before leaving. Even if we had slept together, what right do they have for being angry with us?

I truly thought I was over all of his indiscretions, but clearly I am not. I thought I had forgiven him, but the minute I saw him heading her direction I sprang into action. What if he was approaching them to make amends with his friend? What if I made things worse? Why did I feel cheated on all over again? Why had I not truly forgiven him yet?

Lessons on Losing for those that Want to Win

One day the devil gave a garage sale. He had several tables all spread out with items that he had used for years to divide and devour married couples. On one table he had gossip. On another table he had manipulation. And yet on another table, he had anger and hostility. They could only be purchased as a two-for-one deal. Adultery, fornication, and pornography were a three-for-one deal. A passer-by came through the garage sale browsing and looking around and noticed on a table near the back of the garage sale a strange item on a table marked "for display only, item not for sale." The shopper asked the devil, "Excuse me, but what is this item marked "for display only?" The devil smiled, smirked and grinned demonically and said, "that is my special weapon. When nothing else can get a Christian couple to divorce court I use this and it never fails me. It has caused every divorce this century. That's why I can't sell it." The shopper looked at the item on the table with great fear and asked the devil "What is it?" The evil one laughed, snorted, sneered and wiped his brow and said "this one is unforgiveness!"

The love that your spouse has for you is not perfect, it is flawed. The root of imperfect love produces the fruit of disappointment. With this in mind, it is only a matter of time before your spouse hurts you deeply. In some instances they will hurt you over and over again. They are going to say the wrong thing, do things that you never thought that they would do, and they are going to do things that you knew that they were capable of but prayed would never happen to you. The flawed love of your spouse will drop a hurt on your heart that will bring tears to your eyes, anger to your soul and resentment to your spirit. The pain stings, the hurt is heavy, the embarrassment is real and the only way out of it is for you to forgive them and let it go, but you just can't do it. Keep in mind; the root of marital collapse is always the issue of unforgiveness.

After over 20 years of counseling I have discovered that most married couples are guilty of passive or partial forgiveness. As long as you do not bring up certain subjects, engage certain people or deal with certain issues, you can pretend that you have forgiven them. However, if the right subject comes up, the hurt from the past ends up becoming the pain of the present. There are even times when your spouse has hurt you and you have decided to forgive them and just let it all go, and as soon as you make your decision they go and do the same thing over again and it is like a wound that never ever heals.

In Matthew 18:21-35 Jesus is engaged by Peter who asked Him *"how many times do we have to forgive a person that hurts us, about seven times? And Jesus told him not just seven times but as many times as it takes" (paraphrase).* The word forgive used in this story is an aquatic term used by boaters and fisherman. It means to let up the anchor on a boat and let it sail away. It means to release it. Our problem with forgiveness is often the same problem that we have with giving. We love holding on to things that do not belong to us. Get this and never let it go; you have no right to hold on to your hurt, it belongs to God! We are told in the scriptures to release them to the Lord. Peter says, *"cast all of our care upon Him because He cares about us" (1 Peter 5:7).*

Married couples within the privacy of my office often ask me how does forgiveness work. My answer to them is the same every single time. Forgiveness only happens when you make a conscious decision to look into the mirror of your heart and let the prisoner that's in handcuffs go free only to realize that you are the only one wearing handcuffs. Release the prisoner! Forgiveness happens when you decide to get the wounded patient to the doctor only to discover that you are the one bleeding and need the stitches. Release the wounded! Forgiveness happens when you stand before God and realize that He has forgiven you for all of your sins and He wants you to do the same for others. Now imagine that when you release those that have sinned against you that God tells you, your sins have been forgiven. You see, the only way to be forgiven is for you to forgive. Release the sinner! The key to forgiveness is to release it. Let it go. Put it down and never pick it up again.

Imagine for a moment walking through life carrying a huge box. The box is heavy and it is important to you because there are some special people in your huge box. The people that lied on you are in this box. The employer that fired you is in this box. The person that molested you is in your box too. The parent that let you down is your box and most importantly your spouse that has wounded you deeply is in your box. Your box is huge and your box is heavy. In fact, you have to hold your box with two hands. You never put it down because it is the only way that you can deal with these people so you carry it. You take your box to the store, to church, and the movie. You even bath with your box.

Now imagine healing walking up to you with his arms out stretched ready to help you. Healing can't help you because your box is in the way. Restoration walks up to ready to bless you, but restoration can't get to you because your box is in the way. Peace and joy run up to you excited about your future but neither can help you because your huge box is blocking them from getting to you as well. Now imagine Jesus walking up to you. And, instead of trying to just get to you He takes your box! Your hands are free, you are free, and all of the things that you need to have can get to you because you have given your box of unforgiveness to the only one in the world qualified to handle it, Jesus Christ, Son of the living God!

Forgiving is not forgetting, it is remembering without the pain. You will always know when your forgiveness is real and authentic. You will remember the people that were in your box. But, you will know that Jesus has the box and your past hurt will become your ever present joy. If you want to kill your marriage make sure that you never ever forgive your spouse for the things that they did and did not do. But, if you want your marriage to win, make a decision today and lose the unforgiveness.

The Losers Bracket

- Is forgiveness a struggle for you? If so, why?

- What do you think will happen to your marriage if you refuse to forgive your spouse?

- Based on Matthew 18:21-35 what will happen to you if you don't forgive your spouse?

- Have you ever tried forgiving your spouse and they did something else that hurt you so you held on to your unforgiveness? Discuss what happened.

- What are some sensitive subjects that you and your spouse cannot discuss because unforgiveness makes it nearly impossible? Be specific.

- Are you tired of the pain and the weight of your box? If so, are you willing to let Jesus have it so that you can heal?

The Winners Circle

Take an empty water bottle and place it before you. Now take a sheet of paper and a pen and make two lists. On one side of the paper write this title at the top: "My Sins-Matthew 18:21-35" and on the other side write this title at the top: "My Box-I Peter 5:7." Now take a real look at your own heart and list all of the sins that you know that God has forgiven you for in your lifetime. Be specific and detailed. After you complete that side, flip the page over and complete the side that will chronicle the faults of others to include the things that your spouse has done to hurt you. Also include things that your spouse has not done that they should have done and those things that if your spouse ever did them would crush you. Once both lists are complete, fold the paper up, put it into the plastic water bottle and seal it with the cap.

Now pray this prayer to God:

Lord, you have graciously forgiven me so many times for the sins that I have committed against you. There have been some sins that I have performed more than once, and yet you have never ceased to love me or care for me. Thank you for letting me see and sense what real forgiveness feels like. God, my spouse has hurt me deeply along with so many other people. Yet I know that if you can let me go and forgive me I can and should do the same thing for them. Today is the day of my healing, restoration, renewal and freedom. Lord, as you have released me from my sins against you, I release my spouses' faults, failures and sins against me. With your help and your spirit I forgive them for everything past, present and future that has happened or will ever happen in our relationship. I have placed my sins and the faults of others that have hurt me in a bottle. And, today I am going to trash this bottle, never to see the bottle or its contents again. Lord, just as this bottle will never ever appear in my life again, neither will the hurt that this list that I have put inside of it has brought me. Today I release it and I am free! In the name of Jesus, amen!

CHAPTER 5

LOSE THE NEEDLESS, LOOSE SPENDING

The Story: Winners That Are Losing

Janeen: Manicures, pedicures, facials, massages, power suits, red-soled shoes, oversized celebrity handbags, power lunches, haircuts, hair extensions, weaves, wigs, new cars, new luggage, island resorts, cleaning service, cooking service, child care, elderly care, department store, department store, department store – boutique, boutique, boutique. I enjoy shopping, lunching, hanging, and exploring with the girls. I love being able to just whip out a card and say charge it. My husband Samuel and I both work hard and deserve to enjoy the fruits of our labor from time to time. Plus, he likes me to always look and smell good so I have to stay on top of all of the latest trends.

CHARGE IT!

CHARGE IT!!

CHARGE IT!!!

Samuel: I think it's time for some home improvement. Riding lawnmower, gazebo, change landscaping, add flagstone pavers, fire pit, outdoor kitchen, covered patio, outdoor entertainment system, in-ground swimming pool with infinity edge and waterfall, separate Jacuzzi, jungle gym for the kids, re-pour the concrete driveway, remove all the carpet and lay tile, remove all the formica and lay granite, skylights, knock down walls......Janeen loves it when I take charge and pull everything together. She will have a brand new house before she knows it.

Janeen: Declined? What do you mean declined? I have been shopping here for years and my cards are never declined. You can't cut up my card! I don't care what the company told you. There must be a mistake somewhere because I haven't even reached the limit yet. I need to speak to a supervisor immediately!

Son: Mom, Dad – what's going on? My professor told me to report to the dean's office and when I did I was told that all my classes had been dropped and that I have 24 hours to vacate university housing. I thought it was a mistake, but my dorm room was already packed when I returned. Dad, I'm scheduled to graduate this semester. I can't get kicked out now. They're saying something about not receiving tuition payments and that's why they're dropping my courses. This has to be a mistake, right?

Samuel: Mr. Foreman – what are you doing? Why are all your subcontractors packing up and removing materials from my property? Why aren't they working? Come on now, time is money!

Foreman: Yes, it is. And apparently, you and your wife don't have any more of it. The bank cancelled your loan and is refusing to extend any credit for these projects. I am sorry. Hey, are those your cars being towed away? Wow…

Lessons on Losing for those that Want to Win

If you want to see a feud in a marriage, simply mess up the money. Financial woes in marriage can cause marital wars for any couple. In every relationship there is a spender (this person can spend money like a fire hydrant can spill water) and there is a saver (this person is so cheap they squeak like a rusty wagon wheel). Whatever the case, money issues can be horrible. In many cases, money woes happen when you don't have enough of it, when you have it and you don't know how to manage it, or when you divide it and discover that it divides your marriage.

There are hundreds and thousands of married couples all over the U.S. that struggle because they just don't have enough money. They work hard every day, but somehow still end up trapped in poverty. However, thank God there is a way out. According to the scriptures, the way out of poverty into plenty is to tithe and hustle. Malachi 3:10-14 is a powerful passage in which the nation of Israel has been told how to live life while resting in the blessing of the Lord. It says, **"…bring all of the tithes into the storehouse that there might be meat in my house. And test me on this matter the Lord says. And you will discover that I will open the windows of heaven** *and pour you out a blessing that you will not have room enough to receive. And, I will make the enemy leave you alone and others around you will have to admit that you have been blessed" (paraphrased and expanded).* Poverty can be a curse, but you have the power in your pocket to reverse it!

With tithing in mind, I teach married people to prepare their family budgets with the Lord in mind. Every family should follow a simple financial plan that is 10%, 10% and 80%. The first 10% is your tithe and it belongs to the Lord. A tithe is simply ten percent of your deposit whenever you receive it. If your deposit is $100.00 your tithe is $10.00. If your deposit is $1000.00 your tithe is $100.00. A tithe is a dime on every dollar. It is the Lord's. It is His. The second 10% is your savings for your family. No matter how many bills you have, pay yourselves next. And, lastly live on 80%. When this formula is followed, the blessings of the Lord are soon to flow.

Poverty, however, does not end by simply giving and saving. You must have a hustle. In other words, your tithe is what you owe, but your hustle is what you grow. In most cases, your hustle and your job are two different things. Your job is your place of employment. But, your hustle is what you do for yourself. A hustle is where you take liabilities and make them assets. In short, you take things that you have paid for and make those same things pay you. Keep in mind; a good hustle happens without spending a great deal of money. Simply start with what you already have. For example, if you have paid for a pot and can cook, develop a hustle and cook with that pot delicious meals and charge people for them so that the pot pays you. If you have a car and you can drive, start a small transportation company, charge people for the ride and make the car that you pay for, pay you. If you like buying shoes, your hustle would be to sell shoes. If you like making videos, your hustle would be to video events and sell them. When you tithe (what you owe) and hustle (what you grow), you will see God take what you owe and increase it beyond your dreams because He is going to bless what you grow like crazy! Your poverty will start to become plenty and your money woes will soon be over.

Unlike the families that are trapped in poverty with a lack of resources, there are other families that have an abundance of money, but enough bills and debt to sink the Titanic. In fact, some couples have so many bills that they have undergone a name change. "Work Pay Bills" is their full name or you can just call them "I OWE" for short. Credit card debt, needless spending, consumption, and poor management are enemies in this camp. To make matters worse, in cases like these husbands and wives fight over who spent what and why. There is a way to resolve marital difficulty here. It comes in the form of one word – Budget. Live the creed, "it's not what you have, but it's how you use what you've got." Sit down and make some key decisions about your money usage and include the Lord in your plans. If both parties work, have joint accounts for bill paying and family savings and separate accounts for personal items. And remember this, if you can share beds, you should certainly share banks. Perform plastic surgery immediately. Take a good pair of scissors and cut up every credit card that you have accept one that will be used for family emergencies. Pay-off small debts and then larger ones and learn to live debt-free.

I once counseled a couple that was having intimacy problems. He just could not perform. He had no interest at all in bed time bliss. She would wear cute little Victoria's Secret pieces to bed and he would roll over like a huge ball of dough and snore like he had been working in a coal mine filled with dust. She thought that he was cheating, so they came to visit me. After we got past the surface issues we discovered that the real problem was that she was a shop-a-holic. In fact, when he saw her in bed with a cute outfit on all he could think about was how much that item cost. They worked hard, drove nice cars and lived in a beautiful Victorian style home, but they were smothered in bills. We worked on a family budget, paid off some bills, and she came up pregnant! He didn't just perform, he produced a seven pound, six ounce son. Bills and money woes can kill a relationship, but debt-free living can turn a fire on that cold water can't put out.

The Losers Bracket

- In every relationship there is a spender and a saver. In your marriage, which one are you? Be honest.

- Are you currently happy about your financial condition? If so, what satisfies you? If not, be honest about what is driving you crazy.

- Is God a part of your family's financial plan? Are you a tither? If not, what are you waiting on?

- Credit card debt is a deal from the devil. If you have credit card or bad debt are you willing to get rid of it so that you can start to live debt-free?

- Does your family have a budget? If you do not have a budget, use this moment to visit google.com and type in "developing a family budget" and start by making one today.

The Winners Circle

Debt-free living should be the financial goal of every Christian. The scriptures teach us that the "…borrower is the slave to the lender" (Proverbs 22:7). In short, if you are in debt you are a slave to that debt and the Lord wants you to be free. With this in mind, you are about to prepare your freedom plan. This plan will include three phases. Follow each phase to the letter and live with the expectation that financial solvency and blessing will be the outcome.

Phase I-Make a list of every debt that you owe and write it on a sheet of paper. Include every bill from satellite television to car insurance. When the list is complete add up the entire amount that you need to live debt free. This is the amount that you need to ask God for so that you can be debt-free.

Phase II-Prepare to sow and grow. Go get your check book and write the Lord's tithe right now. Do not worry about any back-owed amounts. Your tithe is not a bill it is a gift. Prepare the tithe right this moment.

Now take your debt and place it in your left hand and your tithe and place it in your right hand and bring them together. Pray this prayer:

Lord, I am testing you at your word today. In my right hand is your tithe, and in my left hand are my bills. I pray right now that your divine provisions flood me and cause me to prosper in ways that I have never prospered before in my life. I know that your tithe in my right hand is not enough to pay off the debts that are in my left hand. This is why I am giving you the tithe right now. In your hand this gift with multiply itself just like the two fish and the five loaves did when you fed the 5000. This tithe in your hand will grow exponentially and miraculously to the point that the bills that are in my left hand will be completely wiped out. Make me be a better steward over the resources that you have entrusted to me. And, I praise you for your faithfulness promised in Malachi 3. Thank you for the open windows of heaven that are pouring me out blessings that I do not have room enough to receive and praise you for making the enemy leave me alone so that my harvest is plentiful regardless to what is happening to our nations' economy. In the name of Jesus Christ I ask it all. Amen!

Phase III-What you owe is your tithe and what you grow is the root of your blessing. You will not see an increase in what you owe until you work in the field of your harvest towards something that you need for God to grow. With this in mind, we want to work in this section to help transform liabilities into assets. In short, we want to take things that you have to pay or have paid for and make them pay you. This will be done by starting a small business in your home. Survey your life and find something that you love to do that you pay for and develop a business with that very thing that can help to earn money that will pay you back. Look for things that are easy to do, cost very little, and will yield great profit. Discuss it with your spouse. If you do not know how to start a small business, simply go to www.google.com and type in "how to start a small home-based business." This guide will help you tremendously and get started right away. Expect God to grow this business because you have been obedient in what you owe Him.

CHAPTER 6

LOSE THE BAD ADVICE OF MISGUIDED PEOPLE THAT SEEK TO GIVE YOU DIRECTION

Story: Winners That Are Losing

Girl, I wouldn't let him treat me like that. I would leave him if I were you. What has he done for you lately? Absolutely nothing. If Spencer truly wanted you then he would be more sensitive to your feelings. It's not unrealistic to want to travel and see the world and have nice things. If he truly loved you, then he would get a better paying job so that he could give you those things. He's just being lazy and set in his ways. You don't need him, Felecia. You need a man that's going to pamper you and shower you with all the trappings of the good life. Isn't that what Spencer promised when the two of you got married? Where is this good life he promised you? So far it's been nothing but bills and babies – you didn't sign up for that. If he has his way, he will keep you barefoot, pregnant, and under his thumb. Felecia, you better divorce that loser and hook up with a winner like I did. You should get with a man like my Donnie; you don't even have to marry him. Sure, he gets mad and pushes me around from time to time, but that's only because I keep messing up. That's my fault. I have to learn to do better so I won't make him have to keep teaching me a lesson, that's all. Plus, he always makes it up to me afterwards. See this necklace? That's making it up to me! It's not wide enough to cover the bruises on my neck, but at least I got some bling out of the deal. Felecia – I'm telling you – this is the way to go. Drop that zero and get you some diamonds, girl! Donnie has a friend that just broke up with someone. The two of you should meet…

Lessons on Losing for those that want to Win

The horror of bad advice, in my opinion, has killed more good marriages than the War in Vietnam, Desert Storm, and the War on Iraq. All too often Christians that are married get their advice from people that have no idea what it is like to live for God in a marital relationship and the end result is always a mess. Please understand that there are times that bad advice can come from a really good person that has earnest intentions, like parents, mother-in-laws, father-in-laws, friends, and close family, but if it is bad advice the outcome will still be the same, a horrible mess will be the end result.

In the movie, "The Color Purple", famed actress Whoopi Goldberg plays the character of Ms. Celie, who is married to one of the meanest men alive, and who answers to the name Mister, a character that was played by Danny Glover. One day Mister's oldest son Harpo decided that he wanted to marry Ms. Sophia. As the movie script opens Harpo visits Ms. Celie (his step-mother) one day for some marital advice. Harpo wanted to know what he needed to do to get Ms. Sophia to obey him when he gives her a command and cook when he says fix a meal. Ms. Celie looks into Harpo's face with earnest sincerity and told him to beat her. With this bad advice in his mind and on his heart he went home and tried to apply the counsel Ms. Celie had given him. The next scene in the movie does not show us what happened, but here's what we do know, Harpo ended up with a swollen black eye and a huge story where he said that a mule kicked him in the face! In short, domestic violence broke out and Harpo got socked in the eye.

I once sat in a private session with a wonderful couple that had been married about six years. The young couple was just starting to have what I call healthy marital tension. It is that segment of marriage where you realize that you really are totally opposite from each other and it is painful and shocking at best. We started the first session with prayer and then I had each of them talk to me openly as if their partner was not present at all. The young lady said that nothing at all was wrong and that they had no need of my services. However, the young man had quite a different story. He opened up and told me how his sweet and shy wife had started to use profanity in their home when she couldn't get her way. He went as far as to tell me how she withheld sexual intimacy from him as a form of punishment and that she would often tempt him and then withdraw herself as if he were a hungry dog chasing a big bone. After both parties had taken a moment to share their thoughts, I asked the young lady how she felt about her husband's comments and she said "I do not deny anything that he said and I don't see anything wrong with it. If it worked for my mother with my Father it is going to work for us too." I paused and asked her specifically, "Your mother told you to do this?" And her reply floored me as she said without any remorse,"yes she did."

Please plant this in your soul and keep it as you seek to make a healthy marriage work, the best advice you will ever get on marriage will come directly from the Bible. In 1 Peter 3:7a God gives men some good advice. It says, ***"Likewise, ye husbands, dwell with them (your wives) according to knowledge..."*** The word *knowledge* used by Peter in the passage comes from the Greek word *gnosko* and it means to be skilled. It means to possess some experience when it comes to a certain issue. In this case, we are talking about ladies. Peter says in a nutshell, if you are going to do well with a sister you have to know how to handle her, which means you can't treat her any kind of way. You must have some skill.

Listed below are seven basic skills that every Christian man ought to know and practice every day of his marriage. Use them to be safe, practice them to be holy and treat them like they are great advice from a super source because they are powerful when used with sincerity and compassion.

1. Never Lay A Hand On Her Except In Love– Simply put, abuse is not tolerated at all. Love your wife in ways that a real Christian man should, but never, ever physically abuse her.

2. Remember This: Chivalry Is Not Dead– Open the door for her, pull out her chair, pay the bill, get the umbrella, notice her, listen to her, give her your undivided attention and handle your business. She will love you for it.

3. Never Compare Her To Any Other Woman– A real lady stands in a class all by herself and knows that she is not a rough draft but a masterpiece. So treat her like she is a one and only, because she is.

4. Remember This: You Can't Buy Her, But Get It Because You Love Her– Please hear this, it's not the amount of money you give her; it's the amount of care and consideration that comes with the

package. If you didn't give it much thought it could cost a million dollars. To a real lady it is still cheap. She wants your heart and not just what comes from your hand. Your time and attention is worth more than your money will ever buy.

5. Never Let Any One Beat You Cheering For Her– Flattery works! Don't take her for granted at all. If she looks good, tell her that. If she has a new look, tell her that you've noticed it. A real lady does not need cheers from you. She can give herself a pep talk in the mirror. But, it always does her good to know that you noticed and you don't mind celebrating it in a way that she can hear you say it. So cheer her on!

6. Remember This: She Is Very Self Conscious Of Her Anatomy, So Love Her Like She Is– No matter how beautiful a woman may be, she always has a part of her body she does not like. Here's some solid news that can help you love a real lady. Love her just the way she is! She knows what she has and what she is missing. But, if you love her like she is you will never miss what she may or may not have.

7. Never Forget That Jesus Christ Is The Real Lover Of Her Soul– All real ladies love the Lord. That's how they have made it through all that they have been through. Keep Him first in all that you do and a real lady will always respect you because you love Him!

Not only is the Bible a great resource of godly relational advice for men, but it is also a goldmine of wise counsel for women. Let's explore some sound Biblical advice for women that want to make their marriages work and grow.

First of all, stay in your place. No, I am not a sexist and please do not rip this section out or trash this book. Hear me out. We are learning from talk show hosts that men and women are equals. This is true in the spiritual sense, but in the human sense it is false. We are not equals, we are opposites. He is male. She is female. He is a man. She is a woman. He is a king and she is a queen. Listen to the Word of God regarding this issue.

"Wives, submit yourselves unto your own husbands, as unto the Lord. For the husband is the head of the wife, even as Christ is the head of the church: and he is the saviour of the body" (Eph. 5:22-23, KJV). God gave men position. He is the head. And, He gave women influence. A real woman defines her man. She never seeks to take his place. In fact, the first real decision any man will ever make is what kind of a woman he wants. She defines him. And he defines a family and a nation. Remember, men are like kites and women are the like wind. If you do not lift him with your influence he will not soar; so stay in your place.

Secondly, watch what you say to him. All too often sisters nag, complain and talk really crazy to good men and it drives them crazy. Words are like bullets out of a gun. Once you say them they cause a whole lot of damage. If you want to mishandle a man, talk crazy to him. The Bible says, *"It is better to dwell in a corner of the housetop, than with a brawling woman in a wide house" (Proverbs 21:9, KJV).* A good man will pass up his house on the way home and skip his house altogether when there is a woman in there who is always talking crazy, raising hell, and giving him the blues. Delilah has been called a "bad girl" of the Bible. But, we can learn some good things from her. One good thing we can learn from her is how to talk to a man. If you want to handle a good man, talk to him the right way.

Thirdly, be patient, prayerful and persistent concerning his rough edges. A real man has some rough edges. He may have some habits that he needs to get rid of, some things that he really should stop doing, and maybe even some things in his life that are a real trip to deal with. But, remember this – he is not a completed project. Here's what the Bible says from the lips of a really good man, the Apostle Paul, *"For the good that I would I do not: but the evil which I would not, that I do. Now if I do that I would not, it is no more I that do it, but sin that dwelleth in me" (Rom. 7:19-20).* Here's some food for thought and some great advice. When a real woman gets her hands on a real man, she can take his rough edges and make something great with them. Peep into the White House right now and you will find Barack Obama. But, look again I say, and what you really should see is what Michelle can do with a handful of rough edges! Be patient and prayerful with your man.

And lastly, always appeal to his manhood. A real man likes a real woman. There is something about a woman that makes him be what he was created to be when she is in his company. Sarah, the matriarch of Abraham knew how to do this well. The Bible says that she *"...obeyed Abraham, calling him lord..." (1 Pet. 3:6, KJV)*. In short, she had a real man and she knew what to do to appeal to his manhood. As a kid growing up we would play basketball all day long. But, when cute girls from the neighborhood showed up to watch us play, we played like we were Kobe trying to win a championship for the first time without Shaq! Why? The presence of those girls appealed to our manhood. Well, manhood in training, catch my drift? In short, if you want a man to be a man you must treat him like a man. Which means this – a sister must be a lady! There's no room for two men in the relationship. If you want him to be what God made him, then you must be what God made you. Always remember this, if you want to be the queen you must crown him as king!

The Losers Bracket

* Have you ever received some horrible marital advice? Where did it come from? Did you seek the advice or did they offer it to you for free?

* When you need solid relational advice who do you normally talk to? Be Specific.

* Have you ever really been confused in your relationship and needed some wise advice and couldn't find any? Did you pray about it? What happened as a result?

* Are you willing to seek and obey godly counsel when you need it? Discuss your honest thoughts here.

- What role do you think that Jesus Christ plays when you feel confused and need direction in your marriage?

The Winners Circle

Plan a session with your spouse. The planned session needs to last for at least thirty minutes. I recommend a nice quiet evening of just sitting on the couch together with no distractions at all. Get a Bible and read the following passages: Psalms 105:4, Proverbs 11:14, 1 Chronicles 16:11, Proverbs 15:22, Isaiah 55:6 and Ephesians 5:21-33. Once the passages have been read openly discuss some of the bad advice that you have received from people about marriage and relationships. When both persons have had an opportunity to share take each other by the hands and make this promise to each other and to God:

Vow of Promise

I promise God and I promise you that I will never, ever again hear, heed, or honor the words of ill advice that come any source. I promise you that I will earnestly and faithfully seek God and His advice only for our marriage. I promise you that my sincere desire is to love you, cherish you, care for you and bless you all of the days of my life. I promise you that I am going to work harder than ever before at handling you with the kind of skill that pleases God and makes you smile. Your life is mine to share, your touch is mine to bear, your speech is mine to hear, your partnership is mine to keep, your eyes are mine to see, your hands are mine to hold, your body is mine to treasure, your spirit is mine to exhort, your walk is mine to witness, your breath is mine to cherish, your destiny is mine to admonish, your weaknesses are mine to strengthen and your treasures are mine to receive. I want the best for you always and I will only seek the best advice possible concerning you…concerning us for the rest of my life.

CHAPTER 7

LOSE THE SELFISHNESS

Story: Winners That Are Losing

His Side of the Story

I worked hard. I threw newspapers while everybody else threw footballs. I helped put food on a bare table while everyone else simply sat and waited for the next meal to appear. When I was finally able to participate in team sports like my peers, I always had to run off to the next odd job so I could have money to buy the jersey, the cleats, the helmet, the gloves, the ball, the sugar, the milk, the flour, the meat; whatever it took to make it to the next day. Middle school, high school, and college were the same. Simply put, I can't remember a time when hard work was not my mantra. I was taught that hard work was its own reward and that I had to protect it at all costs. I learned that lesson quickly because if I allowed someone to pilfer from or take that which I had acquired, my family would go without. As I watched my comrades suffer through one hardship after another, I grew to appreciate those lessons all the more. God had given bountifully and I was appreciative.

The problems began when my wife started staking her claim before we even got married. She insisted on putting her name on everything that was mine before we even said 'I do'. Simply put, I did not like it. What was the big hurry? This never sat well with me because the scales were terribly unbalanced. The cars are mine. The house is mine. The bank accounts with the larger balances are mine. The good credit rating and credit cards are mine. The timeshare is mine. The cabin in the mountains is mine. The retirement accounts are mine. *Everything* is mine. All she had to do was show up and meet my needs: I want 3 squares a day, house, clothes and cars well maintained, and as much lovemaking as we could find time for! That seems like such a miniscule requirement to me, yet all hell has broken loose in my home. My wife was not required to present a dowry as an acceptable 'sacrificial' offering. She was able to pack her bags and move on up to the east side….in my home…..with whatever she had. What she didn't have was quickly provided for her. Everything was provided for her. Isn't that how it's supposed to be? Therefore, when I go to my car, I expect it to be clean and have a full tank of gas. I expect my clothes to be freshly laundered and sorted. I expect the gardens to be tended. I expect the furniture to be polished. I expect all the linens to be fresh. I expect the flooring to be maintained regularly. I expect breakfast and dinner to be freshly prepared every day in the gourmet kitchen. I expect all the bills to be paid. I expect my clothes to be laid out and ready for the next workday. I expect my bath to be drawn. I expect her to make love to me every time I get the notion. Perhaps things would be different if our circumstances were different, but since I am taking care of her, I expect her to 'take care' of me. Why not? She doesn't have anything else to do.

Things have been getting a bit tense lately. She is still insisting on putting her name on everything I own. Why? I love her but this is the status quo and no more changes will be made. I have done everything for her. All she has to do is her part and if she cannot, then she can pack her stuff and go. Everything here is mine and she is just going to have to deal with it.

I would think she would be grateful….

Her Side of the Story

I feel like I am living in a borrowed time capsule from the early 1900s. My husband is so very selfish. How can he not see the need for us to strive to level the playing field? And the two shall become one? That has not happened yet. We are still living in two different realities and it is definitely causing a stir. I find myself resenting him more with each passing day. Had he asked me to marry him only to own me? Was I his puppet or his spouse? I honestly could not tell any longer. I do what I can to meet his demands and keep the peace, but the façade is cracking and he can see the true problem. I do not respect him anymore because of the way he is treating me. Does he think I am going to squander away what he has accumulated? WE are supposed to be building a life together. I have acquiesced and submitted in every way imaginable. I tolerate so much with him because I made a vow and I am striving to keep it. I am almost at the point where I don't want to be here anymore. I knew the fairytale would fade as reality set in, but this is crazy. Since everything here is his, then what is ours? Why am I still here?

Lessons On Losing for those that Want to Win

Selfishness is murder on any marriage. In fact, the terms selfish and separate in marital relationships are synonyms, they mean the same thing. Please hear this radical truth and hold on to it forever; a selfish person in marriage will soon be a separate person in marriage. Your marriage is not just about you. It is not a business deal of equal proportions where the two participating parties split everything 50/50. It is not about how much you put into it and it is not about how much you should get out of it. A Christian marriage is about what we give and not about what we gain, it is about what we plant and not about what we reap, and it is about how much we can share and not how much we can claim.

Believe it or not, the root cause of selfishness is not stinginess it is immaturity. When my daughter Sumone was five years old and her little brother Jonathan was about four, I stopped to observe them playing in the den and discovered why so many married couples find divorce meaningful. Here's how the scene played out between my two kids. Sumone had some chips and Jonathan had some candy. Sumone made a dazzling deal with my son to eat his candy first and then her chips last. Without reading the fine print on the contract my son bought into this concept, hook, line and sinker! When the candy was gone, my son just knew that it was time for the chips. His mouth was ready for chips and Sumone lowered the boom on him like a blitzing line backer rushing the quarter back from the weak side when she said, "I am going to give you some of my chips Jonathan but I didn't say that we would eat them today. You should be good and full because you just ate all of that candy." To the best of my recollection a squabble broke out over those chips and rightfully so. You see, my daughter appears to be stingy (and maybe she was), but more so she was just woefully tricky and seriously immature.

In every healthy relationship three core areas of belonging exist: yours, mine, and ours. In short, it is great to have some things that fit into each area. But, problems arise when these areas leave out the possibility of sharing what we have in them with our spouses. You should never ever have anything in a marriage that you will not share with your spouse. I was once asked to do a wedding in Las Vegas at the MGM. I was so excited for several reasons. One, it was a free trip to the city that never sleeps and second, the wedding was on a Saturday night which meant I could stay the weekend and take some time off. It was wonderful as far as I was concerned. But, my weekend get-a-way got away from me during the final counseling session when I asked the final question of the evening. During every final counseling session before marriage I ask the couple if there is anything that they would like to discuss with me before their big day. When I posed this query to this young couple the bride said, "Well I do have one question for you Pastor." And I said, "What's your question? Fire away…" She said "I have consented to a prenuptial agreement. He has some things in real estate that he does not want to share with me. Do you have a problem with that?" I paused and they waited. I tried to make my answer soft and meaningful but it came out harsh and crushing. I simply told them that God will not bless what He has cursed from the start. If money divides you now it will certainly divide you later. I told them that I could not declare "holy matrimony" over a marriage that is legally divided. I did not perform their wedding, my weekend get-a-way was ruined and that marriage only lasted twenty-two months.

One day while Jesus Christ was teaching on the subject of marriage He made a statement. He said, *"wherefore they are no more two, but one; what God hath joined together let no man put it asunder" (St. Matthew 19:6, KJV)*. When Jesus says that "they are no more two" what He meant was, what has been is no longer. They used to be separate, but now they are one. He did not mean that the two persons would not still have their individuality, personality and distinctive identity. But, what He did mean was that in the eyes of God there would be nothing separating them from being one in Christ, covenant and creation. He then makes it clear what "God hath joined together let no man but it asunder." The phrase "joined together" is very meaningful. It means to fasten with fire.

I once worked at DuPont Chemical Company as a plant operator. While in operations I had time to watch welders do their jobs and was always fascinated with how they could fasten things with fire. They would pull that protective helmet over their faces, light the torch and the work would begin. When they finished, what started as two pieces of metal would be one piece of metal that had been fastened by fire. When Jesus says "joined together" He means what was two is now one and can never be two again. Like two pipes at the plant that have been made one with fire, when a couple takes a vow before God to marry they too have been made one by the presence of God, who is a consuming fire. This is why marriage has no room for selfishness at all. What you have, they have. What they have, you have. And, what you are going to have, they are going to have. It's just that simple. The two are one!

If you struggle with issues of selfishness in marriage, get rid of them before you kill your marriage dead.

The Losers Bracket

- Do you ever feel like your spouse is really being selfish? If so, when? What happens when they are acting this way?

- Are there times when you are selfish? Be honest. When does it normally happen?

- List some things that the enemy uses to divide you and your spouse on. Be candid and clear. What can you do to abolish all of these things?

- If the root cause of selfishness is immaturity, what can you do to grow up in your marriage that will help issues of selfishness go away?

- Every marriage has strengths and growing edges. As a couple that has been fastened by fire, what are some areas that you and your spouse share well in? Be specific.

- What do you think would have happened to us had Jesus Christ been selfish on the cross the day that He died? Discuss your answer.

The Winners Circle

The truth is, all of us are a little selfish in marriage. In the strongest, healthiest, happiest marriages in the world a hint of selfishness exists. We are going to use that selfishness for this exercise. I want you to think of at least one thing in your marriage that you do not want your spouse to have. It should be something that is very dear to you and is completely off limits to them.

I want you to take whatever comes to your mind and I want you to give it to your spouse with a card (homemade or store bought) that simply says "there's nothing that I have that is too good for me to share with you."

Please be mindful that this exercise is not for your spouse. It is for you. Their response to you is of no consequence. The most important thing is for you to share the item with them that at times keeps you away from them. This exercise will take great maturity but it will yield tremendous blessing.

CHAPTER 8

LOSE THE HATRED
AND
LET LOVE WIN

The Story: Winners That Are Losing

I was a beer-drinking, head scratching, football-watching, basketball-ticket-having, tailgating, road-tripping man when she met me. I was tight with my money because I liked to have it so I could spend it when I wanted to. I liked to travel to various locales and have new experiences as frequently as opportunities would allow. I also liked cars and trucks; big cars and big trucks. I like to fix them up and keep them in pristine condition. Why not? I worked hard so that I could play hard. I had no idea that my wife was bothered by any of my 'hobbies' until I rumbled through the neighborhood riding on my new hog.

Initially, I thought she was concerned for my safety. I found it sweet and enduring, up to a point. Sadly, what once seemed enduring soon became disenchanting. My wife's response to my latest purchase was a week-long tirade on the ills of frivolity. *Frivolity?* I could afford to spend all that I spent and still care for her in the best way. There was nothing frivolous about that. Still, I dismissed her concerns and jokingly quipped that she would collect royally if I killed myself on my motorcycle. Before I knew it, she was methodically taking over tasks that I relished doing myself. She began replacing my clothes and shoes (opting for a fashion forward look, instead of the basic traditional look I much preferred), rearranged my closet according to her color preferences, and scheduling couple's activities for every spare moment of time allocated to me. The meat went from fried chicken to chicken cordon bleu, the wine went from drug store to specialty store, and the friends with whom I liked to hang out were no longer invited or made to feel welcome in our home; MY home.

What was happening? I don't like scouring through the closet to find clothing. I like to open the door and see exactly what I am looking for. I don't want to sip wine that costs more than my monthly recreation; I want to knock back a beer wrapped in a partially saturated brown paper bag after a long day at work. And where is the grease? GREASE! Every now and then I enjoy having a few pieces of homemade fried chicken like Mama used to make. Hot, juicy, and deep fried with all of the appropriate sides and followed by a dessert that has enough butter in it I feel my arteries closing each time I take a bite. There was so much junk on that dish she served yesterday that I couldn't even find the chicken! The paper towels were replaced with cloth napkins that I was afraid to get dirty, the gaming system was packed up and sent to the storage room, and a snooty set of people whom I had never met before began visiting regularly for tea, crackers and chess. I want beer, grease, pound cake, games, loud football, and games of pool with my boys.

I know I am a little rough around the edges and that may be a bit much to digest. But I feel like my wife is trying to change me. She is even correcting my speech when my subjects and verbs don't agree. Don't misunderstand me; I love her prim and proper ways. I love that she is demure and delicate, when appropriate. But that is not who I am nor are those qualities which I possess. She compliments me; she smoothes out the rougher edges of who I am. That used to work, but now she is trying to change everything about me.

EVERYTHING.

Lessons On Losing For Those That Want To Win

A seminary professor walked into a classroom one day and asked his class to define hatred. Overzealous shallow hands flew into the air as many of the students shouted out answers without being properly recognized. One young man said, "hatred is the opposite of love." Yet still another said "hatred is not the opposite of love it is the absence of it." And still another from the rear of the room said "hatred is an emotional state of being where anger, hostility and bitterness collide." While hands are flying into the air with alleged answers to the professor's question running rampant he stops the class and says, "All of you are so deep you've missed the core of what real hatred is. Real hatred is simply the covert rejection of anything and is best seen in our attacks against it or our desire to change it to make us happy with it." If this definition of hatred is true and I believe that it is, many of us covertly hate our spouses.

All too often we spend our time in marriage trying to fix, repair, mend, remodel, and do construction on our spouses when the truth of the matter is that the reason we are working to change them is not really for them, it is so you can be happy with them and that is nothing more than covert hatred. I know that your spouse has some annoying habits, but so do you. I am totally aware of the fact that your spouse has some areas that really need work, but as quiet as it is kept, so do you. And it should not go without saying that your spouse has some issues that make living with them tough, difficult and unbearable at times. Again I say, so do you?

Hatred always produces rejection, while real love berths total acceptance. I once was privileged to do a vow renewal celebration for a couple that had been married fifty years without interruption. It was held in a beautiful ballroom of a hotel and it was packed to capacity. The groom stood next to me for a moment but his knees started to hurt so they brought him a chair to rest in while all of his wife's "well seasoned friends" walked down the aisle. Finally the bride walked down the aisle with her cane and a huge grin on her face. When it was time for me to have them renew their vows they silenced me. Instead of renewing the vows as planned they decided to give all of the people their marital wisdom on how to make it work for fifty years.

The old man stood up slowly and said "it took ten years for me to realize that I needed to come home at night, prowling the streets always got me in trouble; it took me ten years to realize that I could trust her; it took me another ten years to understand that she was really trying to help me; it took me ten more years to embrace that fact that she is the best friend that I've had before in my life; and it took me ten more years to know that it's been the Lord loving me through her all of this time. This woman is the best thing that's ever happened to me in my life." By now there's not a dry eye in the place. People are weeping, shouting amen and fanning because the heart of this man had just blessed us. Then his wife says, "I don't really have much to say. But, I will say people do dumb things from time to time. We all have and we all will. But, the true test of marriage is for you to love them while they are dumb and just hang in there until smart kicks in. Don't try to change them, let God do that. You just love them and it will last forever." She reached across me and I said "I'm kissing my husband and I am ready for some cake. Hurry up and cut me a big slice and bring it to me so that I can eat it before my diabetes shot wears off!" All I could say was "Wow!"

The sultry songstress, Tina Turner years ago had the country rocking to her number one hit record, "What's Love Got To Do With It." In her song she called love a "second hand emotion." I could not disagree with her more. Love in our current culture is sorely misunderstood and woefully misconstrued with many other things that have nothing to do with love. Yet, without love hatred rules and marriages fail. Let's take a moment to briefly consider what love is NOT:

Love is not a feeling. If love were a feeling Jesus would not have died on the cross. We can be for certain that Jesus did not feel like a crucifixion the night that He was arrested and beaten. Love is not a feeling. This is why you should never ever make a decision when you are angry or hurt because your feelings are guiding your thought process at that time. It doesn't matter if the thrill is gone or if you feel that your love has withered on the vine, love is still love no matter how you feel about it because love is not a feeling.

Love is not dependent on anything to be what it is. So many people in our day and time need to put love on a crutch for it to be real love. In other words, many people get married because a person has money, a good job, or sex appeal. However, if your love needs anything to stand on or anything to prop it up, it is not love because real love can stand all by itself.

Love is not filled with pride. All too often in marital relationships pride becomes a problem and egos get in the way of progress. When this happens, couples sometimes argue for position and power. Men then seek to train their wives when the Bible says that men should love them. Women seek to lead their husbands when the Bible says they should be submitting themselves to them. Any time love has some pride in it, it is not real love. ***"Charity suffers long and is kind; charity envieth not; charity vaunteth not itself, it is not puffed up" (I Cor. 13:4).***

Love is not abusive. There are far too many people beating and mistreating their spouses under the banner of so-called love. No one in any kind of relationship should be abusing the other party and then telling him/her that it was done in love. Love is not abusive. We are living in an age of abused persons. There was once a time when husbands would abuse their wives, but in our culture the pendulum swings both ways. However, real love does not and will not be abusive.

Love is not exploitation. Everyone reading this book has some weaknesses and some growing edges. However, there are times in marital relationships when spouses learn to use your weaknesses against you and call that love. This is not love, it is exploitation. A spouse who really understands love would never punch their partner's weaknesses, but build on them so that they become stronger and more efficient in areas where they are not strong.

Love is not trying to buy your spouse with things. The story was told of a young woman who was trying to leave her husband because she was unhappy. When the young man found out about it, the news nearly caused him physical illness. He went to his wife and told her that he had bought her the finest of everything that money could buy. She replied, "I don't want things. I want you!" All too often we see love as things purchased and love is not what you purchase.

Love is not something that you find. There was a song out in the early 1980's that had for a chorus "I found love on a two way street and lost it on a lonely highway." Love is not a finding. In fact, if you find it there will come a day when you will lose it, without question.

Now that we have considered what love is not, let's spend just a moment examining what love really is.

Love is a decision. Any time real love exists it is there because someone made a free-willed decision to do it. According to John 3:16 God made a decision to love us not because He had to do it, but because He wanted to do it. His love for us was His decision and that decision is final to this day. Likewise, when we love it should not be because of anything other than a choice that we have made. Love at its core is a sovereign decision that you make. It is something that you chose to do. And the choice is yours!

Love is an action. Love without action is like a television without a screen; it is like a car without an engine; it is like a Burger King with no Whoppers, it is like a church without a cross; and it is like a Bible without the Gospels. If you tell me that you love me there must be proof provided by your actions or your love is vain.

Love is giving. It is possible to give without loving, but it is completely impossible to love without giving. To give is to love; the two are inextricably tied together forever. The Bible teaches us that God loves us. But the proof of His love for us can clearly be seen in what He decided to give for us. God the Father gave us God the Son; His only begotten so that we would always know just how much He loves us. Love is giving and giving is always godly.

Love is patient and long suffering. This is where many of our marriages fail. We are not willing to suffer, suffer and persevere through anything at all. Yet if marriage is going to last forever it is going to require a tolerance level that is divinely given by God that empowers us to remain no matter how difficult the course may be.

Love is kind. There are times in marriage when we can be mean to each other. It is time consuming, unproductive, and ugly. Real love is so filled with compassion until it is intentionally kind.

Love is acceptance. Love in its purest since is open acceptance. When God accepts us He does so in the transitory light of redemption. He accepts us like we are knowing what He is going to recreate. We accept each other in marriage not in light of redemption but in regards to complete toleration. We get to know our spouses for whom they are and learn to love them like they are. That is acceptance and that is love.

Love is God. The divine element in marriage that holds it together is love. This is true because the only one in the world that can hold a marriage together is God. Thus, God is love. When a married couple grows in faith and maturity to love each other not because of what they are but, in spite of what they are not the hand of God becomes visible and love rises to the top. Real love is God's love and it always looks beyond a multitude of faults to see a multiplicity of needs.

Hatred for your spouse seeks to change and rearrange them simply to make you happy. Love accepts them for who they are and leaves the rest to God. Remember this, it is not what you could do with a perfect spouse that counts. It is how much you can really love a flawed one that really matters. Lose the idea of changing your spouse and love them for who they are and God will do the rest!

The Losers Bracket

- What are some characteristics about your spouse that are just not lovable?

- Has your spouse ever hurt your feelings deeply? What happened?

- Have you made a decision to love your spouse in spite of what they have done or are your feelings guiding your path right now?

- People often do dumb things. But, if marriage is going to last, you have to love them past dumb until smart kicks in. Are you willing to do that? Why? Why not?

- Have you ever tried to change your spouse? What happened?

- Love is acceptance. Openly discuss some things in your marriage that have been tough to accept but you have done it.

The Winners Circle

Love is an action word. With this in mind, I want you to choose five random acts of kindness to perform for your spouse. Do them out of love expecting nothing in return.

CHAPTER 9

LOSE THE ADULTERY AND THE CHEATING

Winners that are Losing

I noticed that her cell phone use increased tremendously. Every time I would ask her about it she would just say that she was sending and receiving business contracts that helped to put food on the table. After all she did run a hot-shot company that grossed six figures on an annual basis so I could not question that, but I had a gut feeling something was up. Our intimate life was steamy, passionate and hot, so as far as I knew, everything was cool. Of course, we had our problems but nothing that would make either of us tip out on the other.

Her text messages became needed time away from her family for some badly needed "me" time. She struggled with relaxing from time to time so our doctor prescribed some meds that would help her do that. She was always so happy when she came home from her "me" time excursions. We decided that she needed more "me" time because it was making her smile like I'd never seen. I would do anything to keep her happy and if "me" time is what she needed, then "me" time is what she would have. One day while going through a stack of mail I noticed a credit card bill that had several purchases on it from an out of town stay. We hadn't been out of town and to my knowledge she hadn't either. I had been the victim of credit card fraud before so I called the company and lit into them with vengeance. I had them fax me over the invoices and stay notices and all of them had been signed by my wife!

Several thoughts run through my mind and none of them were holy. I wanted to pray but I was too weak to pray for myself and too embarrassed to ask anyone else to pray for me. I did not say anything to her at all. Instead I sharpened my PI skills and started my own investigative work. When it was time for her next "me" excursion I simply gave her a wad of cash and said "have a great time, love you!" She left with her little bag, but little did she know I took her cell phone, found her pass code and placed a tracking application on that bad boy (it's amazing how much you can learn from watching CSI). I couldn't sleep at all that night as I watched the GPS system track her whereabouts.

She drove to New Orleans, which is only an hour away from our Gulfport residence and checked into the Doubletree Hotel on Canal Street. I did not want to show up too soon so I waited until the next morning to leave the house. That was the longest drive I had ever had before in my life. One part of me said, "go home and chill out, it's nothing, you're overreacting." But, there was the ghetto part of me that said "you're being cheated on so please don't be stupid!" I get to the hotel and tell the receptionist that I lost my key on Bourbon Street and I need another one. She asked me for my credit card and I was more than happy to oblige her. She gave me the room key with a huge smile and said "enjoy your stay."

I took the key from her hand with a great deal of anxiety in my heart and walked over to the elevator. I thought about turning around again but I had come too far to do that. Besides, she wasn't seeing anybody right? I get to the floor that she is on and I began rehearsing my speech of why I am in New Orleans. I decide to tell her that I wanted to surprise her and take her to lunch at Ralph and Kakoo's and then go home so that she could enjoy her "me" time alone. When I get to the door I do not knock. I mean, who does that when you have to pay for the room at the end of the month with your hard earned money for a credit card bill? I opened the door and I hear rustling, shuffling, huffing and puffing. My wife's voice says "this room is occupied, get out!" I turned the corner and I say, "I know that it is occupied, I just want to see by who." She held the cover up to her neck looking at me like a deer caught in the head lights and he just sat there and said nothing. I stood there looking and for a moment I understood why some people are victims of homicide. If I would have had a gun I would have used it, no doubt.

Lessons On Losing For Those That Want to Win

No one gets up in the morning and says "I think that I am going to cheat on my spouse and have an affair today." That's not how it happens. That is not how it works. Adultery and cheating are sneaky demons that start off slowly and end up quickly. Here's how it works. You meet a new person or come across an old one that you wanted to get to know, but couldn't because you're supposed to be in a committed long-term relationship. You make friendly easy going contact, but deep inside you know that the relationship has the potential to go south. With this in mind, you re-label the relationship. When it should be labeled as "dangerous" you label it as a "friendship." From this friendship grows an emotional affair or a third party intrusion that is about to cause major trouble in your marriage. You spend hours talking, too much time texting, and you share things with your "friend" that no one but you, God and your spouse should know. And, because "friends" are cool you touch in a friendly way, but that touch has a feeling attached to it that you know is dangerous, but you don't stop, you keep on going. In fact, you lie to yourself and then believe the lie that you told. Before long it is just a friendly hug and a kiss. From a friendly hug and a kiss comes a real kiss, inflamed hormones, lust, fleshly contact and a "OMG I can't believe I just did that" moment!

Interestingly, the word adultery does not mean to cheat on your spouse, it means to walk away from God. In every relationship where adultery takes place the God that we say we love is forsaken, emotions are torn, feelings are wounded, trust is shattered and the enemy laughs. Many times as married couples face moments like this lots of questions come to mind. "Why is this happening to my marriage?" "What have I done wrong?" "How could they do this to me?" "What is everyone going to think when they find out about it?" And, "Can I ever really love again?" But, while we ask ourselves these questions we miss the culprit, the devil himself.

According to the laws of relational matter, a healthy marriage lives within the boundaries of the rule of 80/20. The rule of 80/20 states that your spouse (at best) can only meet 80% of your needs. This leaves 20% of your needs completely unmet all of the time and this is with a great marriage. Keep in mind, that God leaves some unmet needs in every marriage so that He fills in the gaps of your marriage with His grace. However, if things are already tough you could have a marriage where things are more like 40/60 or even 20/80. This means that your spouse is failing to meet the majority of your needs. Whatever the case, unmet needs are the gateway that the devil uses to divide, devour and destroy marriages every day. Unmet needs leave room in your marriage for the enemy to invite other people into your matrimonial state that are more than happy to meet needs that you are not willing to meet in your spouse and the end result is always cheating and adultery.

A few years ago I counseled a couple that had been hit by the demon of adultery several times. For some reason or another, he just cheated all of the time. Looks did not matter and size was of no consequence. She had caught him cheating numerous times. Finally, she decided to divorce him and send him on his way. But, the Lord had me preach a sermon on relationships the Sunday before they divorced entitled "It's Too Soon To Quit," so they came to see me. We sat in my office and the tears started to flow almost immediately as this woman told me of how she had forgiven this man, time and time again for the same thing. I scheduled an appointment to see him privately and we discovered that he has struggled with rejection issues for years. It started with a father that did not participate in his life to his siblings that labeled him the black sheep of the family. The women that he slept with all had one thing in common; they accepted him just as he was. I asked him why he felt that his wife was rejecting him and he shared with me that she doesn't hug, she doesn't hold hands, she doesn't kiss, and she hates wearing cute bedroom apparel. So in a fit to be accepted he often went wherever he could to get things that home did not offer him. I shared my findings with his wife and asked her to make some small adjustments and she did. They now help teach other married couples how to build an affair-proof marriage and adultery has not been a problem for them since.

In 1 Corinthians 7 Paul teaches the people of God how to build an affair-proof marriage. He says that we should render unto each other ***"...due benevolence..."*** This phrase means to love each other passionately in light of private discovery. In other words, find out what your spouse needs, likes and wants and start doing it. With this in mind, men should remember that intimate love for a woman is different than it is for a man. Men give love to gain sex, and women give sex to gain love. A woman spells love T-I-M-E and A-T-T-E-N-T-I-O-N.

A lady wants your time. She needs to feel a sense of significance and relational value to the man that she loves. Every man on the planet can tell her how beautiful she is but if her husband says nothing she is secretly wounded by it. If a man wants his wife to feel a sense of physical intimacy towards him when the lights are low and the mood is right he must invest himself in both time and attention all day long. It is what I call the "love bank rule for men." This rule simply says, no deposit, no return. If you want intimacy at night, you must make some solid deposits during the day. Call her for no reason, say good morning, tell her that you need her, help her around the house and assist with the kids. A lunch date would be nice. A text message that says, "praying for your day" and a nice phone call that says "I just wanted to hear you voice" will bless you every time.

Sisters keep in mind that men spell love R-E-S-P-E-C-T, M-O-N-E-Y and S-E-X. Men spend their money on what they love. So if he is giving you his money he loves you. And, in his mind, he feels that if he loves you (with his money), then you should want to love him back in a way that he can feel. If you want to keep the enemy away from your marriage, respect your man by treating him like a man and understand that his hard earned money is a simple gesture of love in his mind. So often, sisters feel that their men don't love them or that they don't care because they don't spell love the same way that a woman does. Here's some godly wisdom for you to use that will bless you; know his love language and use it to your advantage. I once had a Cocker Spaniel named Sparky. She was black and cute as a button. She didn't speak English, but she would run in circles, bark and leap when she laid eyes on me. You see, this was Sparky's love language. She didn't speak my language and I surely didn't speak hers but we understood each other and the relationship was great! Now if I could do this with a dog, surely you can do this with your husband. His love language is horrible. He doesn't talk all of the time, he may gripe a bit, he may even hold things in his heart or discuss them with everybody in the world but you. However, if you respect him and listen to his love language, the relationship will work and the enemy of adultery will have no room for ruin in your relationship.

The bottom line is this, if you are involved in a third party relationship that is pulling you away from your spouse drop it like you would if it were a hot rod-iron skillet and give your time, attention, love, money, and respect to the person that you are married to. Adultery and cheating hurt and kill great relationships but love, care, commitment and compassion build marriages that last a life time.

The Losers Bracket

- Have you ever met or encountered a person that you were attracted to since you've been committed to your spouse? Be open and honest about your answer.

- Is there anyone in your life right now that you know could be a threat to your marital commitment? What makes them a threat for you? If there is someone that is a threat, what do you have to do to eliminate the existing threat?

- In a healthy marriage your spouse can only meet 80% of your needs, leaving 20% of your needs unmet. How do you handle the unmet needs in your relationship?

- The only way to keep the enemy out of your marriage is by rendering due benevolence, one to the other. Is there anything stopping you from rendering this benevolence to your spouse? If so, what can you do to eliminate it?

- Men and women have completely different love languages. What is your spouses' love language?

The Winners Circle

This is going to be an exciting exercise, I promise. I want you to have an affair! Have a full-blown, heated, passionate, fleshly, lustful, remarkable affair; an affair that you would never ever forget. It is going to take time, energy, effort, communication, hard work, raw effort, money and moments where you are sworn to secrecy. But, it is your assignment nonetheless. Please note that I did not say that you were going to cheat and I did not say that you were going to commit adultery. But, what you are going to do is engage your spouse in heated conversation, romance, passion and godly love like you never have before.

Here is how this exercise is going to play out. In every adulterous relationship, several elements exists that the devil uses against us. For the sake of this exercise, we are going to take them all back and use them for God as you get to know your spouse over, and over, and over again and seek to render unto them due benevolence. With this in mind, you are to do all of the items listed below. Please keep in mind that affairs take time so this assignment may take several months to play out but do it and I promise it is going to bless you:

- Contact your spouse and ask to meet them

- Spend hours texting and talking just trying to get to know them

- Find out who they are, what they like, most importantly what they need

- Listen, laugh, love, lust, chat, talk, flirt

- When they play hard to get, work harder to get what you want from them

- Buy gifts, make time for little visits

- Kiss again for the first time

- Go on a date(s)

- Plan a hotel stay to include everything

- At the height of the affair recommitment your marriage to God by reading I Cor. 7:1-8 and praying with your spouse

- Keep the affair going...with the Lord's hand on your life it never has to end!

CHAPTER 10

LOSE THE BAD ATTITUDE AND THE HARMFUL DISPOSITION

Story: Winners That Are Losing

He barks at me all of the time. He gets on my nerves. Every time I look at him I am reminded of how he treats me. I feel more like an indentured servant than his spouse. Things changed more than I realized they would when he asked me to be his wife. I feel like I am expected to step into unreasonable roles to fulfill the marital contract. Sometimes I feel like the maid, the chambermaid, the cook – the reincarnation of his mother. I know I have intentionally been ugly to my husband as of late, but only because he has isolated me so much this past year. I loathe coming home because I know the cycle is going to start all over again. He barks at me and I scowl at him. That has become the norm in our home.

The ironic thing about it is I overheard him telling his Mother (of all people!) that I am unappreciative and unruly. Really? I should have snatched the phone and told her he was selfish and unfulfilling. That would have shut everything down. With all of the negativity between us, I don't even remember the last time I enjoyed being in his presence for any reason. There used to be a time when I could count on our intimate times to restore the focus on solidifying our bond; not any more. As his demands continue to increase, I am finding everything about our intimate times to be lacking and falling short in every way. You know, love hides a multitude of sins – but gosh.

The latest blowup occurred when I got home from an extended workday only to find the kitchen littered with dirty pots, pans, and dishes strewn all over the place. That atrocity was eclipsed by the swell of testosterone-filled cursing in the game room. All of the usual suspects were assembled and having a field day. There was no regard for cleanliness; primarily because he told them to leave their items where they were… "my wife will take care of all of that." Really? Initially, I tried not to embarrass him by responding when I overheard that statement, but he continued and he allowed them to continue to pile it on for the next several hours, so I decided to busy myself elsewhere until their evening was done. That plan seemed to work fine until he 'summoned' me to clear away their mess. I entered the room as he was apologizing for my laziness. Needless to say, all hell broke loose and all the fellas quickly got scarce; that night ended with us on opposite sides of the issue and on opposite sides of the house.

I tried once more to converse with him about what had transpired and his response was to bite my head off. I had failed him, yet again. I was not living up to my wifely potential. I was not taking my responsibilities seriously enough. I heard him. I listened. I acquiesced, again. Perhaps I had unrealistic expectations was truly the problem. I tried things his way, but that did not work either. I found myself resenting the ground upon which he stood. The climate in our home was spiraling out of control and I had a great deal to do with it. I no longer had the desire to attend to his needs – none of them. I resented him, his family, his friends, everything and everybody associated with or connected to him. I felt that a gross misrepresentation had taken place and I wanted it to change or I wanted out. We were both professionals with demanding jobs. I was not inclined to come home and engage in indentured service to suit his needs. What about my needs? I did have a few, but none of that mattered. I resolved to take matters into my own hands. I tried to converse with my husband once more. I did not like the things he said to me, but I knew it was important that I listened and heard him. I wanted him to listen and hear me. I needed him to hear me. Instead, he dismissed me. Nothing was ever the same from that day forward. Something (else) was now broken in our marriage. The respect factor was missing and I had not yet resigned myself to living the rest of my life without it. I am no queen, but coworkers and even strangers treated me better than this. Didn't I deserve better from my husband? Hadn't I earned it?

Lessons on Losing For Those That Want To Win

Godly marriage is not for immature people. It is for those that are mature enough to handle what comes with it while possessing the right attitude. Being mean in a marriage is a royal waste of time and it is seriously childish. It takes energy, planning, time, and often times extra effort just to do it and no one wins in the end. Not to mention that when you hurt your spouse you actually hurt yourself. The wrong attitude directed at your spouse is often unhealthy, ungodly, unnecessary and unappreciated by them. Most importantly, the attitude that you invest into your spouse is the attitude that you should expect from your spouse. If you don't want to reap it, please don't sow it. And if you don't desire what you give for yourself, then never give that to the person that you are married to. Remember this, the golden rule of any real relationship is to treat others like you would want to be treated.

In St. Mark 16:17 Jesus says, *"these signs shall follow them that believe, in my name they shall cast out devils..." (KJV).* Devils are evil spirits that come from the abyss. They cause division, distraction and destruction. But, Jesus gives us a method for handling them. We have the right to cast them out. A better way to say the same thing is to say that real Christians have God's authority to send demons home. And, since they live in hell we can rightfully say "to hell with that" to demonic figures. I mention this because there are ten dangerous attitudes that are demonically driven that often destroy good relationships like termites reduce beautiful homes to rubble. Consider these horrible attitudes below and when they arise in your heart and in your marriage resist them and prayerfully commission them to hell where they have come from.

The Attitude of Uncontrolled Anger. Being angry is not a sin. All of us will see moments of personal anger in our lives. But it is during moments when our attitude is raging that the enemy is most busy. Fix your attitude so that even if anger arises we do not sin. This attitude when unchecked leads to domestic abuse, verbal abuse, physical confrontations and divided families. Replace anger with love, it wins every single time.

The Attitude of Blame. Marital difficulty is not just your spouses' fault. Demonic activity always follows the same pattern. They want you to do what Adam did in the Garden, blame someone for your mistakes. Remember this: blame points fingers but love lends a hand. If all you can see is the faults of your spouse replace fault finding with soul searching and ask the Lord to work on you until you are right and when God starts to work on you He will also start to heal your spouse.

The Attitude of They Come First. This is a slow marital killer that works every time. This is perhaps the sneakiest attack of the enemy used against marriages today. No one wakes up and says "I am going to put my marriage, family and focus in the wrong place." But, life, necessities, work, kinfolks, friends, church, kids, and other stuff can pull us so far away from our spouses until we become perfect strangers living under one roof. Replace "they come first" with this model: God first, family second and everything else later. This will put the enemy in his place and bless your marriage.

The Attitude of I'm Sick of You. If you have ever said these words pause and ask the Lord to forgive you. Your spouse is an extension of the Lord's blessings in your life. For you to become sick of them is to say that you are tired of the Lord and that should never be the case. Keep this in mind, if you tell your spouse things like this you are killing your marriage and the devil gets a huge laugh. Replace 'I am sick of you' with the attitude that says 'I need you.' I need you is powerful enough to send demons running back where they have come from.

The Attitude of This Marriage is Over. This is the lead killer in marital failure. This is a deadly attitude and it must be destroyed. Your marriage is not over in glory until one of you dies. If you are not dead it is not over and it is just that simple. Replace the attitude of this "marriage is over" with the attitude of God is not through with us yet. Lean towards God and trust Him with your marriage and He will do what no other can do.

The Attitude of I Will Never Forget What You've Done To Me. This may be the deadliest attitude of them all. The reason for this is because its root is purely demonic. We are most like animals when we seek revenge. We are most like humans when after being hurt we give up on the person that has hurt us. But, we are most like God when we forgive. Replace the attitude of 'I will never forget what you've done to me' with 'I love you in spite of your mishaps, mess-up's and mistakes.' When husbands and wives do this God smiles, the enemy frowns and marriages are restored.

The Attitude of God's Way is Good but My Way is Better. This is the devil's ace in the hole when he really wants to land a solid destructive blow to a great marriage. The enemy will force an attitude upon you that you that will make you think that the answers to your marital success are in your head and not in God's hand. Marriage was made by God, for God. So since He created it, His way of doing it should be at the forefront of everything a married couple does. Replace your way with His way. His way works!

The Attitude of I'm Giving You a Chance to Change. When marriages struggle, people often stay in the marriage waiting for their spouses to make some changes. Please receive this in all humility; in most cases what you see is what you get. If there are going to be any changes made in a marriage they will come first from within you. The change from within you will promote change that happens all around you. Your walk with God is the real key to marital change. Nothing else! Replace the attitude of giving your spouse a chance to change, to asking the Lord to help you make the changes that you know that you need to make.

The Attitude of What They Don't Know Won't Hurt Them. Not long ago an 18-year-old girl knocked on my best friend's door. No one in the house knew her. But, she said "may I see the man of the house?" My friend stepped to the door and the young lady said to him, "I'm graduating from high school this year and I thought I should let you meet me. I am your daughter." Of course, the house was in an uproar, they took the paternity test and she was indeed his child. Here's the point of this segment: your secret will not always be a secret so talk about it. Replace the attitude of 'what they don't know' with the attitude of 'let's be honest with them and tell them.' It is always better to discuss it early than it is for it to come out later. Keep in mind, deep dark secrets in a marriage are just like landmines in the field. Eventually they get stepped on and it causes damage every single time.

The Attitude of Love as a Game. Toys are for kids but marriage is for adults. This is not a game. It is not a contest. It is a covenanted commitment to Jesus Christ that should last forever. If you find yourself playing over your spouse with someone else, playing with your spouses' feelings and emotions, playing with their heart and soul, get rid of that foolishness immediately. Replace the attitude of playing the game of love with the attitude of growing in grace so that your spouse has all of the love that they will ever need from you. Remember, marriage is not a playground it is a battle ground and there are times you have to fight for your marriage and family just to keep them together. Your marriage is worth the fight, don't let it go!

Attitude in marriage is vital. A dangerous attitude that last too long can kill it. But, the right attitude filled with godly love can restore and heal it. If you have a bad attitude lose it today.

The Losers Bracket

• Bad attitudes kill marriages every day. When you look inwardly, are there any places in your life where you know that you really need an attitude adjustment? Please be honest.

• There are ten dangerous attitudes listed in this chapter. How many of the ten have you seen in your marriage lately? How are you dealing with them?

• Never plant an attitude into your spouse that you do not want to reap as a harvest. What are some bad attitudes that you have planted in your spouse recently?

• If you have been married for a while you have already undergone some major attitude changes. What role did the Holy Spirit play in helping you to work first on yourself?

• Godly marriage is for mature believers who can handle it. A great attitude reflects your level of maturity in the faith. If you had to rank your level of maturity on a scale of 1 (childish) to 10 (very mature) where would you rank? What can you do in prayer and principal to grow more in grace each day?

The Winners Circle

Changing your attitude towards your spouse takes time, work, effort, prayer and at times struggle. With this in mind, this exercise is designed to be a month long program. For the next thirty days you will engage yourself in radical random acts of kindness that will require an attitude adjustment on your part. Here's how the month and the exercise will play out. Privately take a calendar of any month of the year that you chose. You may use the one in your cell phone, iPad, kindle, or hard copy calendar. Mark the month as "Radical Acts of Kindness Month." Each day of the month should include a kind act, word or deed from you towards your spouse. No matter how your spouse responds, do it. This exercise is not for them, it is for you. At the conclusion of your day during the 30 day "Radical Acts of Kindness Month" read the prayer shared here:

Prayer

Lord, when I think of your kindness towards me my eyes swell with tears, my heart warms with joy and my soul shouts in jubilation. You have been so kind to me. It is my prayer today that you would work through me to extend your kindness to my spouse. There are times Lord when I do not treat them or speak to them as I should. Forgive me please. Today I humbly ask that you would work through me to show my spouse your love and compassion through a Radical Act of Kindness. I know that the enemy will try everything in his power to hinder this moment of marital love. But, the devil is a liar and you deserve the glory. God help me love my spouse today in words, thoughts, and deeds in ways that make you happy. Finally Lord I sincerely ask that you would adjust my attitude towards my spouse over the next thirty days so that what I start doing this month continues onward for the rest of my time on earth with my spouse. In the name of Jesus Christ I ask it all. Amen!

Conclusion

Losing is never easy to do, especially when you have been working hard at winning all of your life. In fact, when students lose because they have failed a course tears of hurt are not uncommon; when athletes lose they sit silently in a melancholy mood and ponder what caused them to lose the game; when investment bankers lose they are known for falling into deep bout of depression that can last for months; when laborers lose their jobs due to corporate layoffs or downsizing it can be crushing; and when campers lose their way on an overnight trip fear strikes a chord in their soul because dangers are hidden and hope seems futile. In short, losing hurts. But, all losing is not bad. In fact, there are times when losing can bring joy, victory, healing, and restoration.

Marriages fail when the men and women involved in them refuse to lose. But, when husbands lose families win, when wives lose marriages survive and when covenanted couples in Christ lose for His sake the kingdom of our God reigns supreme. Here's the blessing of this book, we lose so that we can win! Never forget this. This work has touched on a few basic areas that most marriages will need to lose in so that their marriages can survive and thrive, but there are many, many, many more that we need to discuss. It is my prayer that they can be covered in the next book, "Marriage is for Losers, vol. II."

In closing, Christian marriage was designed by God so that people in the world could see a living model of how Jesus Christ feels about His church. Your marriage is not about you, it is really about the God that you love and the faith that you live. Make up your mind to lose so that generational blessings can flow from your heart through your children and grand children and for many generations to come. Marriage always requires a complete sacrifice, but losing is worth it when the victory of winning is the guaranteed outcome. Remain steadfast in your marriage and sacrifice whatever it takes to make it work and remember this, Marriage is for Losers.

Dr. John R. Adolph is available for speaking engagements and public appearances. For more information contact:

Dr. John R. Adolph
C/O Advantage Books
P.O. Box 160847
Altamonte Springs, FL 32716
info@ advbooks.com

To purchase additional copies of this book or other books published by Advantage Books call our order number at:

407-788-3110 (Book Orders Only)

or visit our bookstore website at:
www.advbookstore.com

Longwood, Florida, USA
"we bring dreams to life"™
www.advbookstore.com

Celibacy is for Fools

A foolproof guide designed to help, hope and heal singles
That dare to do relationships God's way

By

Dr. John R. Adolph

Dedication

This work is dedicated to the finished work of my personal Lord and Savior Jesus Christ on the cross at Calvary. His love for his bride, the church, has been the core influence of this book.

To my loving, wonderful, beautiful wife, Dorrie (Baby), for her 16 years of love, care, friendship, commitment, patience, toil, support and prayers and to my two wonderful children, Sumone Elizabeth and Jonathan Rayshawn.

To my mother and father, Rev. Seymour V. and Barbara J. Adolph for their life-long example of marital commitment.

To my mother-in-law and father-in-law, Pastor Vincent and First Lady Albertina Washington of Gardena, California who perpetually model marriage for our entire family to embrace.

To my siblings and their families, Pastor Seymour V. Adolph, Jr. (Jenny), Daisy Adrienelle English (Curtis), Ron L. Adolph (Wandy), my nieces, nephew, and relatives that have always been an ever present support system of love all of my life.

To my single saints that travel with me everywhere I go that dare to share with me their relational struggles, everyday strains and spiritual issues, Candace White, Eljon Stephens, Joshua M. Daniels, and Damien Williams.

To the many single saints at Antioch Missionary Baptist Church of Beaumont, Texas that are relationally real and spiritually determined to do relationships God's way.

To every single believer that seriously desires a lifestyle that pleases God.

To all of the sexually active singles that knows that it is not right to engage in sexual intimacy without first being married but sin on a regular basis.

To all of the single saints that have tried celibacy and failed.

To every single person that has been hurt, wounded, wrecked, and nearly ruined trying to love people that would not love them back.

To every single celibate saint that is committed to remain abstinent as a sign to the world that there are those present that love God more than anything that this world has to offer.

Table of Contents

Foreword

The only way to adequately describe "it" is by calling it "the big IT." The world loves to talk about "it." Hollywood consistently unleashes movies filled with "it." Kids (just like I did) snicker and joke about "it" on playgrounds and in school hallways. Parents become uncomfortable even considering when might be the appropriate time to bring "it" up to their growing, pre-pubescent children who are constantly being sent a myriad of messages about "it." The "it", of course, is the s-word. You know: s-e-x. A couple of years ago, I had a teenager say to me as I was observing his Sunday school class, "Pastor Noble, in this class we always talk about the devil and temptation, especially drugs and alcohol. But when is our teacher going to talk to us about, um, you know, sex? I've asked, but Bro. Sunday-School-Teacher doesn't want to deal with it. And, in my opinion, that's the big one. Yeah, sex is the big one. Since he doesn't want to talk to us about it, is there a book you could recommend that we read on our own?"

Enter the author of this book and my long-time friend, John Adolph.

John understands very well that age-old assumptions about sex – assumptions that were once considered bedrocks of our puritanical, prudish, head-in-the-sand society – can no longer be considered safe assumptions. Sex before marriage is as common and unquestioned now as abstinence *until* marriage *once* was. Face it: those days of hushed tones, taboo subjects and nothing-but-the-missionary-position are long gone. Sex is here; sex is hot; sex is, well, sexy; and it's not going anywhere anytime soon. John has taken the mantle upon himself and has forged ahead with a boldness that I have come to expect from him. In fact, as I read the preview copy he sent to me, it dawned on me that John uses the word sex more in the first three paragraphs than most Christians ever hear in a lifetime of attending church! With disease and sickness and ignorance ever on the rise, someone has to take off the clergy collar and cassock and boldly go where few pastors have ever gone before. I have known John since we first met in the bookstore of the Morehouse School of Religion years ago (don't you dare ask how *many* years), and I can honestly say that he is broad shouldered enough to broach "it", tackle "it", deal with "it", and let the chips fall wherever they may.

Be forewarned that we may not all agree upon every conclusion drawn nor upon every exegetical device employed within these pages, but *shame on us* if we allow disagreement to hinder us from at least engaging this most important discussion within the body of Christ. I applaud and salute my friend for his willingness to lead the way in educating us all about God's will concerning this gift that God has given us; you know…"it."

Dr. Derrick-Lewis Noble
Pastor, Crenshaw United Methodist Church
Los Angeles, CA

Introduction

Make no mistake about it, sex is everywhere. It's on television, the Internet, billboards, magazine covers, advertisements, commercials, infomercials, and found in bookstores. It is mentioned in music, seen in PG-13 rated movies and please, don't even mention R rated films. Sex is everywhere you look these days. But that's not the problem. Here's what's wrong.The world is loud about sex while the church is silent on the matter. So most of what we know about the subject of sex comes from sources that have nothing to do with the God who designed us to be sexual beings at all.

Just take a moment and think about it. Most men have their first sexual discussion around fellows in a locker room or just some guys hanging out while watching a beautiful lady in jeans pass by. That's when you hear all of the comments that leap from the frontal lobe of our testosterone filled heads like a diver jumping into a pool from a platform thirty feet high. And women, contrary to popular belief, are quite the same. They talk too! Don't let anyone fool you on this one. If the walls of most beauty shops could testify and if pots in the kitchen could grab a microphone and sing a song we would hear them sing a concerto in E flat about sex.

If we would only be honest, we have heard the news about sexual positions, sexual fantasies, and sexual escapades. We've heard about safe sex (taught in most school districts across this country), oral sex, great sex, and sad sex. We have been informed on near sex experiences, drive-by sex that was unplanned and unintentional, sexting on cell phones where people use modern technology to send pictures and videos of sex, Internet sex and pornography. We hear the news about encounters that lasted for minutes, to stories where things got heated and lasted all night long. We get all of the information about what to wear that looks sexy, what fragrance or perfume to wear that smells sexy, and what vitamin supplements to take that make it last longer. The discussions go on and on.

Not long ago, HBO featured a special on four dynamic comedians entitled "The Four Kings of Comedy." Posthumous funny man Bernie Mac had people laughing to tears as he cracked jokes about sex. However, as I watched people laugh themselves to tears I thought of the many people that I have seen weep because they have been wounded, tattered and torn in sexual relationships that went bad simply because they had no idea what God really designed sex for. Yes, sex was designed for the blessing of reproduction between a man and a woman. But, it was also given to us by the Lord to be shared between a husband and his wife for the purpose of becoming one in His sight through a covenant with Him that we should keep for a lifetime of love.

With this in mind I must present to you a radical spiritual truth that you may already know, but for the sake of clarity and redundancy I must say it again: if you are not married and you consider yourself to be a Christian you should not be having sexual relations at all. Wait! Don't close this book yet. Don't trash this work because it is going to bless you in the end. Much if not all of the advice you've ever been given about sex has come from sources other than the Bible. This is why this book is so very special. Since God created us to be sexual beings let's hear from Him on the subject.

When the Apostle Paul set aside worldly wisdom for the wisdom that comes from the Lord he called himself and others like him a "...fool for Christ..." (I Cor. 4:10a). The word "fool" that he used to describe us with comes from the Greek term "moros." We borrow our word moron from it. Now a moron in a secular sense is someone that has been declared mentally retarded. However, in the Greek sense it means that I have put the worlds way aside and I am living my life God's way. It means that you have made a decision that your way is okay, but the Lord's way is best. At its root, it means that you are living to make someone else happy instead of living to simply satisfy yourself.

This is where the core, crux and center of this book presents its chief argument. The only way for a single saint to be saved and celibate in a culture where sex is everywhere is to be a complete fool for Jesus Christ. Thus, the real deal here is, celibacy is for fools. Celibacy is for the believer that will stand flat-footed and declare "I am living for Jesus Christ no matter what everyone else has to say about it! Call me a fool if you must, but I am a fool for Christ!"

This book is not being presented to you without personal testimony. I started having sex at the age of 13 years old. A group of guys in my neighborhood convinced me to engage a girl from the "hood" who would be happy to oblige me and so my ignorance of God's plan for sex started. Don't talk about me or judge me. Some of you reading this book started before I did and have continued doing it wrong even though you know what is right. At least I stopped at the age of 24 years old. I'd had enough and I wanted something real and lasting. For three years and eight months I was a fool for Christ and I loved every moment of it. I share this relevant truth with you about my past because if God could heal me of my ways, He can do the same thing for you.

This book is designed to be a helpful guide to every born-again believer in the Lord Jesus Christ who sincerely wants to do your relationships His way. For some of you reading this work it will be the greatest relational step in the right direction that you've ever made in your life. No one else will take this step for you so take it for yourself. Each chapter will present lessons that are filled with information, practical ideas, and Biblical resolves that should empower you to be both saved and celibate. I pray that this book blesses you in reading it as much as it blessed me writing it.

Chapter 1

I'm A Fool For Love

Let's go ahead and clear the air as we share in literary fashion one with another. There is sex that either honors or dishonors God. Think about it for a moment. The improper use of anything powerful can cause more harm than good. A gun can protect you, but in the hands of an idiot it could kill you. Prescription pills in a bottle can heal you, but if you take all of them at one time you will more than likely become seriously ill. And, if you have a car that runs, it can get you where you need to go, but if you have someone that lacks skill behind the wheel driving, you may crash and never see your intended destination. Like anything else that is powerful that needs to be handled with skill, so it is with sex. Physical intimacy is powerful and the only way for it to bless you is for you to know how to use it.

I once engaged a group of singles at a church conference and I asked them to talk openly about sex. At first the room was silent. Some of the people in the room looked at me as if to say "is the preacher about to go pornographic on us in here?" But, I stood my ground. Silence ensued so I said again, "let's talk about sex." A few people got up and walked out of the room, but the vast majority stayed. One young handsome man just said, "Reverend Adolph I love it!" With a Bible in my hand I openly affirmed him by telling him that God made him to like it. In fact, I told the entire group that God wanted them to enjoy it so much that He wanted them to give Him glory for it while they were engaged in it. They all cracked up laughing. The classroom settled down, but no one else jumped into the conversation. Since I had one taker on my hot topic, I asked the young man that said that he loved it what he loved about it. He said with vigor in his voice, joy in his soul and a sheepish grin on his face, "I love the positions!" To the best of my recollection the room was in a complete uproar for at least ten minutes.

I waited for them to calm down and that's when I lowered the boom. I said that's going to be my lesson subject for today. Since this young man likes positions, I am going to teach about "Making Love in the Right Position." I told them open their Bibles and let's talk, learn and share. Today when the subject of "love making" comes up, people call it "the nasty."It can suggest everything from two women in bed together, two men in bed together, an unmarried man with a married women in bed together, and two unmarried people in bed together just to name a few. The point is, our culture has been making love in the wrong position so long until we no longer see this beautiful God given act of love the way that it was meant to be shared.

CNN recently did a documentary on the teenage sexuality of middle school aged kids in the US and the findings were staggering. Five out of ten were sexually active by the age of 12; seven out of ten had encountered some form of sexual contact by the age of 12; and, nine out of ten had encountered some form of sexually explicit material on the Internet, such as nude photos and pornography. In short, what they are learning is love from the wrong position. A chapter like this one is godly and necessary. In fact, if you are not married and sexually active, yet you stand under that banner of Christianity, you are in the wrong position. If you are married and you are involved with anyone except for your covenanted spouse, you are in the wrong position. If you are involved in any behavior that would displease God and bring harm to you and your family, you are in the wrong position. But, if you are married, sharing your faith and your future with a spouse of the opposite sex, then according to scripture you are indeed making love, and you are making love in the right position.

The Bible says, *"Now concerning the things whereof ye wrote unto me: It is good for a man not to touch a woman. Nevertheless, to avoid fornication, let every man have his own wife, and let every woman have her own husband. Let the husband render unto the wife due benevolence: and likewise also the wife unto the husband. The wife hath not power of her own body, but the husband: and likewise also the husband hath not power of his own body, but the wife. Defraud ye not one the other, except it be with consent for a time, that ye may give yourselves to fasting and prayer; and come together again, that Satan tempt you not for your incontinency. But I speak this by permission, and not of commandment" (I Cor. 7:1-6, KJV).*

When the subject of making love in the right position comes up, what position is the right position in the eyes of the Lord? There are four positions that this chapter will guide us through. These are the positions that honor God and bless those that are faithful enough to be a fool for Jesus Christ.

Position #1-Spiritual Compatibility

Hear this word of warning. Be careful around people that do not love the Lord like you do. Be cautious around anyone that does not have your same level of commitment. Be careful entering a relationship with someone that will tell you that they do not do the church thing. It is dangerous and my advice for you is to run! In the passage Paul gives us an elliptical of the cause. That is where the given truth is not openly stated. Here is that given truth, people should always be equally yoked together. This means that both of you are saved and have the same desires spiritually. If you are with someone and they tell you "it aint gonna hurt just this one time...." That's the wrong position. If you are near someone and they tell you "Jesus won't mind if we bump and grind...." That's the wrong position. If you are in a relationship with someone and they tell you that they want to marry you, but you must have sexual intercourse with them as a test run to make sure that you both like it..." That's the wrong position. If you are having sex with a person that you feel is a significant other, 'shacking up,' or doing the "let's go and get a room thing..." That's the wrong position. If you are with someone that is really good looking but they tell you "I don't believe in Jesus Christ perse...." That's the wrong position. And, if you come across someone that is in church but will put his or her religion down to "hook up"for fleshly motives....that's the wrong position. What makes love great is when both persons (male and female) are in Christ Jesus and He is in them. And both people really, truly desire to please God mind, body, heart and soul. That's the right position and it pleases God.

Position #2-Serious Commitment

Listen, love is NOT a game! I do not know who did it, but somebody made love a game and it's been killing us. The end result of the game is

CHAPTER 1

LOSE DIVORCE AS AN OPTION

The Story: Winners That Are Losing

Nag, nag, nag! Wash the car, clean the garage, mow the lawn, trim the hedges, put your shoes away, hang up your suits, find the remote, close the door, open the door, pick up the dry cleaning, go to the store, kill the mosquitoes, spray the flies, feed the dog, investigate things that go bump in the night, sit through chick-flicks, put it down, pick it up – gosh! When did I sign up for all of this? I should have known it was going to be a mistake to marry someone so stubborn and strong-willed. At least when I was single I was my own boss. All of those same things still had to be done, but I was the captain of my own ship which meant that I could do them when I wanted to --- if I wanted to. Now, I go to work every day, make the money, bring *some* of it home, then start the extreme 'honey-do' cycle all over again every single day in my house. I'm the king of this castle and I'm being treated like a servant by the queen. None of this was listed in the job requirements section of our marriage vows. I want a divorce.

Nag, nag, nag! Wake him up, put him to sleep, gas up the car, sweep the garage, tell him what to do, pick up after him, hide the *!#% remote, pay bills, drop off the dry cleaning, cook three squares a day, keep extra everything on hand for the boys on any given game day, clean the house, keep every TV in the house tuned to the sports channel, take care of *his* kids, pacify *their* mamas, put up with baby-mama-drama, take care of *his* mama --- gosh! When did I sign up for all of this? I should have known it was going to be a mistake to marry someone that had baggage but no dolly. At least when I was single I was my own boss. All of those same things still had to be done, but I was the only 'Diva on Deck' which meant that I could do them when I wanted to --- if I wanted to. Now, I go to work every day, make the money, bring *most* of it home, then start my chores all over again every single day in my house. I'm supposed to be the queen of this castle instead I feel like a chambermaid; a housekeeper; a servant.

gods of the underworld and the people were honoring these strange gods by embracing strange sexual encounters that please these strange gods. But, Paul says if you want to make God happy let a husband have a wife and let them touch. This act honors God and it blesses the man and woman involved. It is not the "nasty" as the world describes it, but it is the "Holy" as God designed it.

Imagine a moment what it would feel like to make love to someone and not get up feeling guilty because the act was sinful in the eyes of the Lord. In fact, try to think of preparing to touch someone intimately but before you come together you hold hands and say "Lord we honor you with our worship as we touch. You know that we honor you because we share with each other a covenant of everlasting love. We love you Jesus. Amen!" Can you see that? This is the position that every believer should be in because sex is an act of divine worship that pleases God and it only happens when both people are totally submitted to Jesus Christ.

Position #4-Set To Fight Against Satan

Temptation is the word used by Paul to describe what the enemy does when he seeks to get us out of position. The Greek word is pi-ros-mos. It means to put two elements in a test tube to see how they react with each other for the purpose of devouring them both. When you decide that you are going to only make love in the right position you can look for the enemy to send someone your way for him to tempt you with. In most cases, they will be someone that will grow on you and ultimately someone that you can say you've fallen in love with. But, watch your position. Satan does not play fairly and he will use everything that he can against you just so that you can fall, fail, and flounder.

When I started my celibate lifestyle I just knew I had my flesh under control. I was so in control of things that I had become critical and judgmental of others. I was like a spiritual police officer looking for people that made the slightest mistake so that I could judge them. Late one night during my holiest hour of sanctified Bible study I received a phone call from one of my female sin friends of the past. She came over wearing a beautiful wrap dress and with some sweet smelling perfume on. To make a long story short, I failed the test. I went to Flunkersville in a tacky car, with a low back tire and a bad muffler. I sinned and sin I did. Now here's what is so bad about the whole thing. I lost six months of celibacy and had to start over. Not to mention the fact that I was sleeping with the enemy and never knew it. She was so sweet and nice. However, anyone that pulls you away from your walk with God is acting on behalf of the enemy no matter how nice they may seem. It was a satanic plot to begin with and I failed the test. From that failure subsequently came three years and eight months of tests that were passed. My conclusion about the matter was that Satan cannot make you sin, but he can make temptation convenient. Stay in the right position and you will experience victory every time.

The classroom that was filled with singles at the church conference was completely engaged in the dialogue about making love in the right position. The young man that said he loved all of the positions raised his hand and asked the question "if I am out of position how do I get back in? I want to do it right." While his hand was raised I asked the entire group one question. How many of you if given the opportunity to make love in the right position would take it? The entire group lifted their hands and the tears began to flow. It was then that I told them about the God of forgiveness. The greatest news of the day is this God has a holy habit of letting people start over! I John 1:9 says to us that "…if you confess your sins God will forgive your sins and cleanse you from all unrighteousness…" (Paraphrase, KJV). A revival broke out and everyone in the classroom left in the right position.

If it worked for them it will work for you too. All you have to do is want it badly enough to ask God for it and receive it. And always remember, sex is not bad, especially when you know how to make love in the right position.

Chapter 2

I'm a Fool for Dating that Makes Good Sense

Almost everything that we know about dating comes from sources that have nothing to do with God. The chief reason for this is due to the fact most marriages in the Bible were culturally prearranged. So the idea of dating as it is seen and practiced in our culture rarely existed. However, there is a way to date without losing your mind, messing up your morals, having children out of wedlock, or shacking up and leaving the relationship feeling bitter, hurt, disgusted and dumb if it doesn't turn out to be someone that you will marry in the future.

In 1997 Joshua Harris wrote a book entitled, "Kiss Dating Goodbye." In his work he openly expresses complete disenchantment with dating as our culture practices it. His feelings should not go without note in this chapter because in almost every relationship that we hear of today dating almost always implies some form of sexual intimacy. I recently engaged a group of young men in my barbershop on the subject of dating. I asked one handsome fellow how many women he has dated in the last year. He told the entire shop with pride about eleven. One of his friends asked him how many of those girls that he dated had he had sex with. Silence filled the shop. One young lady said, "Tell the truth. Don't lie to us because Pastor is sitting in here." He smiled and said ten. All I could say was "Wow!" The entire shop laughed, but I thought to myself, in our culture dating almost always means sex of some sort. It implies that we kiss, rub, touch, fondle, send pictures via cell phone, or send steamy text messages that involve sex via cyberspace.

The world's system of dating may involve sex, but as believers that are in love with the Lord the way of the word will always light our way. Here's a truth that you need to hold on to: dating does not have to involve sex. You can date with your mind clear, your pants on, your dress down, and your morals intact. In short, I believe that you can date and be saved at the same time. Dating for a Christian that is living a celibate lifestyle involves four key areas of relational matter that if practiced well can lead to a closer walk with God and lifelong friendships that are healthy and godly. Let's look at all four areas as this chapter unfolds.

AREA #1-First Level Relationships "Randoms"

Randoms are people that you are just getting to know. They are prospects that exist from a distance. They are the people that you meet that grab your eye. It doesn't matter where you've met them, whether at a game, online, through a friend, at church or in the mall; there is something about them that makes you say "I noticed them." Under the guise of this area of any relationship you should meet new people, talk with discretion and simply feel them out. In other words, treat this new relationship just like you would an interview, because that's exactly what it is. Examine the person by just talking to them. Interviewing is to Randoms what rice is to gravy, they should always go together. Develop a list of questions that you would want to ask someone just to discover what kind of person they are. Here's some questions that you should always ask:

1. Are you a believer in Jesus Christ? (If they answer no to this question, seek to share Christ with them. If they do not desire a relationship with the Lord....RUN!)

2. How committed are you to the Lord? On a scale of 1-10, rate your commitment to the Lord, 1 being sorry and 10 being awesome.

3. Do you believe in sex before marriage? (If they answer yes to this question....RUN!)

4. What are some of your lifelong goals? Where are you headed in life? (If they are headed nowhere they will want to take you with them....RUN!)

5. What do you do to earn a living? (Money is not the most important thing, but it is certainly a core thing. Love is one thing, but it does not pay bills!)

6. Where are you from? Who are your people? (Make sure that you ask this question because you may be talking to your cousin and not know it.)

7. How important is your family to you? Do you have any children? If so, tell me about them. How do you feel about them? (Trust me on this one, if their family is not important to them, neither will yours be.)

8. What are some things you love to do?

9. What are you really looking for in a relationship? What are you expecting? What do you bring to the table? (Listen carefully to the answer to this question because it could knock you off of your feet.)

10. If you could ask the Lord for just one thing, what would you ask for and why?

This is just a few good questions that you can ask, but please feel free to add to this list when you start to develop your own questions. As it relates to dating, first level relationships are nothing more than interviews for the position of spouse. There are millions of people that are available, thousands that quality, hundreds that fit the mold, a few that you may be interested in and just a handful that will actually get an interview. Treat your handful as interviewing candidates by asking good questions. Run if you see or hear anything that sounds crazy. Trust me: you will save yourself some heartache in the end.

By the way, don't just ask questions during this state of the relationship, but be careful about what you do and don't do as well. Here is a small list of some do's and don'ts that you must include in phase one of a relationship:

1. Don't go on a date or have them over to your house; it is way too soon. The person could be a maniac and could cause you more harm than good.

2. Don't discuss your thoughts with them via text message, social media or anywhere else in cyberspace. It makes you look simple, cheap and easy. Talk over the phone.

3. Don't introduce them to your children (if applicable) or your family. It's way too early for that.

4. If you talk to them and you really like them a lot, don't tell them that just yet. A skilled artist doesn't paint fast. They move slowly to avoid frivolous errors. You do the same. Just because you like them does not mean that they like you.

5. If you are not interested, treat them like you would like someone to treat you. Be honest with them, be compassionate, but be on the move. Don't send mixed signals.

Keep in mind, interviewing should last at least two weeks, if not longer. This gives you time to size them up, figure them out and screen them well. If you are really feeling the person and you see that the feeling is mutual, move forward with the friendship.

Area #2-Second Level Relationships "Potentials"

Let's be honest: most "Random's" don't get through the interview process. Many of them get cut. This may sound harsh, but it's true nonetheless. Some of your newfound friends may have some potential. A "Potential" is that person that you have interviewed and they have really piqued your interest. In other words, their interview went well. When you hung up the phone you said to yourself, "They've got some sense and it seems that they are headed in the right direction." If that is the case and they are feeling the same about you then that relationship is a second level relationship and it has some potential.

At this level of a relationship, please know that everything that looks good to you ain't good for you and everything that glitters is not gold. You are at this stage of the game because the interview went well and you can sense that this individual seems to have something special going for them. Now this is where things get juicy and go to the next level. You interview Randoms, but you investigate Potentials. That's right! When a Random becomes a Potential, you should put on your CSI outfit, pull out your Dick Tracy hat, Sherlock Holmes utility pack and start investigating like crazy. Be nosy. Figure out who that person is and listen to everything you hear about them. Of course, everything you hear will not be true. But, looking at the fruit around the tree will tell you what kind of tree it is. Even if the fruit hits the ground and rolls it will tell you what kind of tree is nearby.

The more you investigate the more you will find. Look at what you have discovered and weigh it carefully. Of course, no one is perfect, but if your investigation turns up information that is bad, don't lie to yourself. Put it down and walk away. However, if the investigation turns out things that are good, then move forward with skill and prayer. A good potential seems to have what it takes to become the right one, so take things to the next level. Listed below are some things that you should do with someone that has potential:

1. Find some time to interface with them. Start going on dates with them, but do not let them pick you up from your home just yet and vice versa. Meet them wherever you are planning to go.

2. No overnight trips. Save those for when you get married.

3. Talk, look and listen like you are a private detective working for the CIA.

4. Keep your morals in check. If you are really starting to have feelings for them, never be caught alone with them.

5. Do not introduce them to your family or children yet (if applicable). The reason for this is that like Randoms every Potential does not make the cut either.

6. Find out what they would really want out of a relationship with you. Listen attentively at this point. If you sense that all that they really want is sex….RUN!

7. Pay careful attention to calling habits. If calls are not consistent it means something is wrong.

8. Watch how they treat other people, especially those that are closest to them. People will eventually treat you the same way that they treat others. Therefore, what you see is what you will get.

Area #3-Third Level Relationships "My Boo"

One day while sitting in my office I overheard a conversation between my kids and a young man who was nearby. My daughter Sumone asked this young man if a certain young lady was his "Boo." I was so shocked I didn't know what to do or say. I told her to come here and to mind her business. Afterwards, I had her take me to the relational school of the current culture. I asked Sumone what was a "Boo?" And she said, "Daddy, that's the person that you are seeing when it is just you and them." It made enough sense to me to put it in this book, so I did.

All Potentials are not Boo's. Your Boo is the person that started off as a Random, but passed the interview. They became a Potential, but made it through your harsh investigation and they are now your agreed upon exclusive relational friend. Okay, let's clear the air right quick. By friend, I do not mean anything other than that. In short, your Boo should not be your sex partner. However, it is the person that you have an agreement with to only date them and them only.

For the sake of clarity, all too often when we get to this stage of the relationship things start to become attached. You know each other pretty well. You're used to hearing their voice on a daily basis. This person has a space in your life. Feelings get involved. You're emotionally entrenched. And then, you start to desire this person physically. Please know that this is perfectly normal but not spiritually legal. Don't do it yet! There is no covenant present. This is where the problems come in. People often treat Boo's like spouses and the end result is children born out of wedlock, scratched up cars, soul ties, credit card bills for gifts bought that you couldn't afford, hurt feelings, relational stress and moments where your Boo makes you boo-hoo hard enough to make use profanity and lose your mind. Here's some good advice, stay focused!

The only reason why you make a person your Boo is for the purpose of intimacy. However, the intimacy is not meant to be personal, but spiritual. You want to be intimate with the Lord while in the presence of your Boo. In short, pray together about each other. You see, you interview Randoms; you investigate Potentials, but you fast and pray with a Boo. Of course you spend time with them, but that time should be shared seeking God about the relationship and asking God for direction. As the Lord reveals things to you both in prayer look for revelations and confirmations. If the Lord pushes you away from that person, obey and make them a lifelong friend but know that God has someone else for you. If the Lord presses you towards that person don't be fearful, be faithful and move forward with them knowing that your Boo will be the person that you share you future with.

Area #4-Advanced Courtships "The Right One"

When the Holy Spirit confirms for you that your Boo is the person that you will share your future with, if you're a woman, wait for a formal proposal. This may seem a bit old fashioned, but that's where I am. I believe that a man should go to the father of a young lady and ask him for her hand in marriage. If she doesn't have a father any man of influence in her life. After he does that he should spend some money on a ring and humbly ask her hand in marriage.

Now here's the exciting part. You are now engaged and you can tell the world that the Lord answered your prayers and blessed you with a soul mate! In other words, you have met a lot of "nice-one's" but the Lord has given you the "right-one." Now here's something to shout about. Wait on your wedding day, rush to your honeymoon suite and let the Lord show you what real sex was designed to feel like! Dating can be done right when you do it God's way.

Chapter 3

I'm A Fool for Waiting

Not long ago we took a trip to Atlanta and while in the Olympic City we decided to purposefully encounter some of their southern cuisine. What did we do? We found our way to Gladys Knight's "Chicken and Waffles." We had been traveling all day long and we could smell the food outside but could not go in. You see, there was a line of people trying to get in that ran outside of the door onto the side walk. We had to do something that none of us like to do. We had to stand in line and just wait.

Let's cut through the chase and admit it. Waiting gets on our last nerve. But, all of us are waiting on something. Single believers in many cases are waiting to be married. Sick people are waiting to be healed, children are waiting to be teenagers, teenagers are waiting to be grown, grown folks are waiting to be wealthy and have someone take care of them for a change, sisters are waiting to exhale, older people are waiting to be respected, college kids are waiting to graduate and our friends in Haiti are waiting on relief. Everyone is waiting on something.

The healing news for today however is this: there is someone that you can wait on and when the wait is over you can shout these words with passion, purpose and power, it was worth the wait! In Psalm 27 David brings healing to every waiting soul when he gives a word of illumination to those in darkness by declaring "The Lord is my light and my salvation..." He moves from illumination to consecration. He tells the reader that he only desires one thing from the Lord and that is to "...dwell in the house of the Lord all of the days of His life..." After the word of illumination and consecration he then downloads a word of elevation when he shouts, "...when father and mother forsake me then the Lord will take me up..." In other words, when what was supposed to hold me up collapses the Lord shall keep me in His hands. But, he concludes with a word of hope and healing for everyone that is waiting on the Lord he says, ***"Wait on the Lord, be of good courage and He shall strengthen thine heart, wait I say on the Lord!"***

So what is the real blessing in waiting on the Lord? Let's explore these ideals together in light of being both saved and celibate.

One of the greatest blessings found in waiting on the Lord is to know that your portion is from above. The reason why waiting on the Lord is so worth it for a single saint, is because what God wants you to have is greater than what you thought you could have ever received. The word "wait" used in the text is quavah and it is in the piel stem and the imperfect mood. It means to look to a larger source to have your needs met. Like a child looks to a parent so we look to God. The only problem is that you do not get what you want when you want it. So the only way to get it is to wait for it. The shouting news of the day is everything that you need is available through your source and the storehouse is full. In other words, God has your portion! Healing, He has your portion. Deliverance, He has your portion. Direction, He has your portion. Your soul mate, He has your portion. Your portion is in His hands so wait on Him.

Secondly, waiting on God is worth it because your perseverance comes from within. You will never gain strength hanging around with weak people. This is why you always want to be found with saints that are strong in the faith that have been through hell and hurt, and came out of it with a testimony and a scar. It is because you discover that the God that is within their soul kept them and gave them strength. David says it this way, "...be of good courage and He shall strengthen thine heart..." This should read like this, "...and He shall make you tough and cause you to endure from the inside." Let's be honest, waiting can make you want to quit. But, when you feel like giving up, talk like the people that have made it and say "I am going to hold on to the Lord until my break through comes!" And when you do this, strength comes from the inside to keep you and cause your waiting to be your blessing.

Lastly, waiting on God is worth it because your plight is in His plans. Listen to this and put it in your spirit, the reason why you need to wait on God is because what God wants for you is much better than what you could have ever wanted for yourself. In other words, God's plans are much better than your plans. So, learn how to wait! The Psalmist ends the verse the same way he begins the verse. In short, this Psalm will bless you going and coming. It says, "Wait on the Lord.....wait on the Lord." It is written twice because the Hebrew language does not have punctuation marks. There was no way to shout a phrase, so they just wrote it twice. Look at this four-word phrase as if it were written like, "WAIT ON THE LORD!" Why? Because the Lord is ordering your steps and right now where you are is not a moment of conclusion, it is a step in your progression that will end in a celebration of victory. So wait on God, because it is worth it!

We waited for a good while at Gladys Knight's restaurant. But when we got ready to leave people were walking out of the restaurant slowly with doggie bags in hand and toothpicks dangling from their lips. And one dear friend said to me as we boarded the bus to go to the hotel, "It took a while, but it was worth the wait." Now if waffles from Gladys were worth waiting on, surely the God of heaven is worth your wait too. Wait on the Lord and know that your needs will be met through Him.

Chapter 4

I'm A Fool for Hurtful Relationships that Crush Me

"For Women Only"

Not long ago while in Kroger I spoke to a sister that was on my aisle. She looked up at me with a grim disposition and a partial smile on her face. When we got to the checkout stand she said, "You're Pastor Adolph aren't you?" And of course I answered yes. She then asked me an ontological question that has theological roots and sociological fruit. Here's what she asked me while getting a basket full of grocery to feed her two kids "Why do I keep getting hurt? I am a good sister and I desire a committed relationship, but I just keep getting hurt over and over again."

I have 5,000 Facebook Friends and I have noticed that when it comes to relationships many of my female Facebook Friends will list themselves under the "Relationship" category in a very interesting way. They do not say that they are engaged or that they are dating, but they list their relationship status as "complicated." In my opinion, this is just another way of saying "I have been hurt before in relationships and I am trying to make sure that I don't put myself in that position again."

I cannot count the number of beautiful women that I have counseled in the private chambers of my office that have been seriously wounded in a relationship, trying to love a man that will not love them back nor give them the love that they deserve. The tears that run from my office could compete in a marathon. The hurt is real and it runs deep. But, all of the damage is not the fault of a horrible man that sought to take advantage of a good woman. In fact, most of it is not. All too often good women get hurt because of relational error and lack of applied moral principle that leads them to the abyss of relational hell every single time.

Please know that such a story is not uncommon. There is a woman found on the pages of Holy Writ that got hurt and she too was a good woman. Here is how the story flows, *"And he (Abram) went in unto*

Hagar, and she conceived: and when she saw that she had conceived, her mistress was despised in her eyes. And Sarai said unto Abram, My wrong be upon thee: I have given my maid into thy bosom; and when she saw that she had conceived, I was despised in her eyes: the LORD judge between me and thee. But Abram said unto Sarai, Behold, thy maid is in thy hand; do to her as it pleaseth thee. And when Sarai dealt hardly with her, she fled from her face" (Gen. 16:4-6, KJV).

There is no doubt that Hagar was a good woman but she got hurt for the same reason that many good women today are wounded in relationships. She ceases to be celibate and she becomes sexually involved with a man that was good to her but was not good for her. Let's take a moment and explore the facts and factors that show us why some good sisters get hurt.

The first reason that good women get hurt is because they fall in love with a man who is what they like but is not what they really need. There is a documentary on YouTube that features five beautiful women that are well educated, financially solvent and well-to-do. Their problem is that they cannot find a compatible mate. As I listened to them discuss what they wanted in a man I was clear on one thing. Not one of them knew what to look for. Please hear this, what you like and what God wants you to have are not always the same thing. In fact, in many instances they are quite different. This is why a believer that is seeking a spouse should be celibate and prayerful. If you get your feelings involved with a man that is not right for you then you have created a soul tie. This happens when your mind, body and soul are attached to someone that it should have never ever been attached to in the first place. They are dangerous and trust me when I say that you lose when you are involved with them every single time. You lose your time, your resources, your energy, your peace (the relationship almost never ends peacefully), and your walk with God is always compromised. Hagar makes a common mistake that I have found in good women everywhere. She falls for a man that is husband material, but not tailored by God for her needs. My dear sister, if God has not made a man a husband before you get to him a woman (no matter how good she is) will not make him one. If you cease to walk with God, you will ultimately walk away from Him and the end result is relational pain and anguish. Things may glitter for a little while but they are going to end up tarnished.

Secondly, good women get hurt because they settle for temporary satisfaction instead of demanding a lifetime of love. The real truth is that sisters are often guilty of settling. Please remember this, if you learn to settle you will always get what you have settled for, so don't be upset in the long run for having the crazy man that you have decided to settle down with. Settling is very dangerous and it makes a woman look both dumb and desperate. Dumb simply because you know that you are doing it while you're doing it. He's not the one, but since you've turned your brain off you move onward anyhow. And, desperate because instead of waiting on the Lord in a way that will keep you sane and celibate you move forward with your feelings in one hand and your underwear in the other, only to get dropped again after heated moments of temporary intimacy and the sharing of bodily fluids. This is not God's way. Hold to your standards and never ever compromise them for any reason under the sun. This is both attractive to real Christian men and a blessing to you in the long run.

In his hit movie "Act Like A Lady, Think Like A Man" Steve Harvey swings at this Biblical notion with what he calls his "90 day rule." Harvey contends that you should make a man wait at least 90 days before having sexual relations with him. I contend that Beyoncé is right: if you like what you see then put a ring on it! Hagar settles for a man that will never be her husband; a disaster from the start. But, like Hagar many women settle for different reasons. Some women settle for abuse (verbal, physical, emotional, and financial) while enjoying great sex; some settle for less fulfilling sex just to have a piece of a man nearby because we've been told that a piece of a man is better than no man at all, some settle for the husbands of others, and some settle for a man that is not saved, but is good looking. Still others settle for a man that is average looking but has money. Even more settle for a brother that is broke and is headed nowhere and wants to take you with him and because you long for companionship like a crazy woman you settle for it. And, there are even more that settle for a man that will never make a full commitment to you, so he wants you to act like a wife but doesn't want to behave like a husband. So you end up being the special day woman or a part-time love. Keep this on your heart at all times: if you learn to settle you will always get what you have settled for.

Thirdly, good women get hurt because they give too much of themselves too soon. Okay, let's just say it: we are having a promiscuity problem. This is not the case in every circumstance. In most cases, however, the problem is sex too soon. Here's the best advice that I could give any godly woman that desires God's best for their lives; keep your dress down, your pants up, and never put yourself in a position for your moral virtue to be compromised. This means no overnight stays (at your house or his pad), no late night visits, no hotel rooms, no cruises and weekend get-a-ways, no shacking up, no nightcaps (not even iced tea). Respect yourself and he will respect you for it. If Hagar had done this, her life would have avoided the hurt of having a baby out of wedlock for a man that would never marry her in the first place. Celibacy works because it makes a man pray, think and decide. Besides all of that, if a man needs a license to ride a motor cycle he should have a license if he wants to go for a ride with you. No free rides allowed. No test drives. No test runs. Remember this; if you treat yourself like a treasure the men that dare come near you would treat you like the treasure that you are. Treasure your body and if he wants to play, get a license and make him stay! This is why celibacy blesses you. It moves the notion of temporary satisfaction and replaces it with lifelong love that comes to you as a result of your commitment to Jesus Christ.

Lastly, good women get hurt because they allow themselves to be engulfed in relationships that are bad from the start. The worse lie that you will ever believe is the one that you convince yourself is true. Do not ignore the warning signs in a relationship and then become unglued when things fall apart. If he is abusive while you are dating, he is going to continue this pattern but things are going to grow worse. If he cheats on you before marriage, you can be sure that he will cheat on you if you marry him. If he is led by his mother before marriage, you just married his mother and she is going to run your house too. If he is crazy while you are courting, he is going to be a maniac if you marry him. Every relationship has warnings signs. Heed them! Hagar knew that Abram was married, but she ignored all of the signs. She got caught up. Please hear this, women often get hurt because they get caught up. Open your ears and listen. Open your eyes and look. Get on your knees and pray. Jesus put it this way, "...watch and pray..." In almost every case, women who got hurt knew what they were dealing with before they got hurt. For some crazy reason they thought that things would be different with them or would somehow start off rough and end up smooth. With this in mind, some of the heartache that women face is self-inflicted and can be avoided if celibacy is practiced and godly moral principle is kept in place. Remember, whatever a person does with you they will soon do to you. It is only a matter of time before it happens. Don't get caught up in something that you can see the warning signs of ruin from the beginning.

Here's a great question for every real single woman. Are you sick and tired of having your feelings hurt? If you are, then give your life to God and abstain from sexual contact until He provides a husband for you. Celibacy may sound foolish to the people of the world but it makes good sense to the sister that understands that waiting is worth your while all of the time. God will not hurt you like others already have. He is waiting on you to turn your face, soul, and heart completely to Him and live for Him like you never ever have before. Let the Lord heal you today and never ever go back into the lifestyle where temporary lust tries to erase the lifetime of love that you were born to have and surely deserve.

Chapter 5

I'm A Fool for being the Best Woman That I Can Be

"For Women Only"

I know that you have heard the old cliché that "men are like buses. When one leaves another one comes along." Author Michelle Hammond, however, raises an even better interrogative for her best-selling book while using this mantra. She puts it on this order, "If men are like buses how do I catch one?" This chapter is not written to suggest that every woman is looking for a man. Neither is it being shared to suggest that all single women are desperate. But it is being written so that single sisters can know what to be before the right man enters the picture.

All too often beautiful single women catch the wrong bus (more than once in some instances), while other women stand on the wrong corner trying to get a good bus in a bad place (catching brothers in the club and meeting them at the pub), and still others get on the bus hoping for it to go in a new direction when it travels the same old route (you know, the same man from your past that you revisit hoping for something new, but you get what you got the last time you were with him). Here's the hard to swallow truth of the matter: relationships can be very difficult in this day and time. But there is great news found in the pages of holy writ for sisters that are waiting on the right one to come along.

The Bible shows us a portrait of a woman that is the perfect model of a sister that is a diva who really has it all together. Here's what the book says, *"Who can find a virtuous woman? for her price is far above rubies. The heart of her husband doth safely trust in her, so that he shall have no need of spoil. She will do him good and not evil all the days of her life. She seeketh wool, and flax, and worketh willingly with her hands. She is like the merchants' ships; she bringeth her food from afar. She riseth also while it is yet night, and giveth meat to her household, and a portion to her maidens. She considereth a field, and buyeth it:*

with the fruit of her hands she planteth a vineyard. She girdeth her loins with strength, and strengtheneth her arms. She perceiveth that her merchandise is good: her candle goeth not out by night. She layeth her hands to the spindle, and her hands hold the distaff. She stretcheth out her hand to the poor; yea, she reacheth forth her hands to the needy. She is not afraid of the snow for her household: for all her household are clothed with scarlet. She maketh herself coverings of tapestry; her clothing is silk and purple. Her husband is known in the gates, when he sitteth among the elders of the land. She maketh fine linen, and selleth it; and delivereth girdles unto the merchant. Strength and honour are her clothing; and she shall rejoice in time to come. She openeth her mouth with wisdom; and in her tongue is the law of kindness. She looketh well to the ways of her household, and eateth not the bread of idleness. Her children arise up, and call her blessed; her husband also, and he praiseth her. Many daughters have done virtuously, but thou excellest them all. Favour is deceitful, and beauty is vain: but a woman that feareth the LORD, she shall be praised. Give her of the fruit of her hands; and let her own works praise her in the gates" (Proverbs 31:10-31, KVJ).

You see, the woman in the passage is ready for a relationship and her bus comes along. But, what should a single woman do if she really has a desire to have God send her a good man? Here are some practical points from this passage that should empower every sister that will use it.

First of all, you have to handle yourself like a precious jewel. I am so tired of watching women handle themselves like trash but want a brother to treat them like a treasure. Get this, my friends: a man will treat you like you treat yourself. Here's what the verse says, "...her price is far above rubies..." In other words, her system of personal value cannot be calculated with money. Not long ago I was invited to attend an all white celebrity bash with Deion Sanders in Dallas, Texas. Dorrie and I went and things were great until I looked around the room. It really hurt my feelings. The sisters there were not wearing enough clothes to wad an aspirin bottle. It was like a meat market that said, "Thighs $2.00 per pound, breasts $2.75 per pound and legs free with a purchase of $100.00 or more!" Yes, there were star athletes in the room. But, if you treat yourself cheaply then so will he. Please, dress like you're a treasure, talk like you're a treasure, walk like you're a treasure and make him treat you like you're a treasure.

Secondly, you have to handle your money like a banker. Okay, this may seem harsh, but I have to add this to the gumbo while I am standing over the pot. You do not need a man's money if you have your own. Why spend anytime digging for his gold when you can dig for you own? This virtuous woman in the passage spots a piece of real estate and she buys it with her own cash. Now this is a real diva. Keep this in mind, I know that many women work everyday (both married and single), but if you are still broke at the end of the day, all you do is work to pay bills. It's not what you have it is how you use what you've got. It makes no sense to have a Dooney and no cash, a Benz and no maintenance agreement, and a diamond tennis bracelet and no savings account. Believe me when I say, real men are not intimidated by a sister that can handle her business (boys are, and that's another lesson). A real man finds an educated, business savvy saved sister seriously sexy.

Thirdly, you have to handle your kitchen like a chef. I am not trying to start any trouble here, but I have to say this because it is true. Cooking is not a sin. Never before in all of my life have I ever seen so many culinary deficient women. How can you say that you really want a good man and you cannot boil a sausage or make some toast? Now for those of you who call this kind of teaching sexist, take the matter up with the virtuous woman in the text. She cooks for her husband, her kids and the whole house. Yes, the way to a man's heart is through his stomach and the way to a man's soul is his mind. You need both in this day and age. I have a good friend that put it on this wise, "Men don't just want thighs under the table, he wants some thighs on the table!" If this is not your cup of tea here's what I suggest; turn on the cooking channel and just watch it as you fall asleep at night. Some of what you see will slowly become what you do. And if that does not work for you, catch your grandmother by the apron and ask her how she cooks her cabbage, corn bread, yams, greens, fried/baked chicken, black-eyed peas, mashed potatoes, green beans, bacon, eggs, grits, pancakes, and pound cake! Let her school you and I promise you that it will be worth your while.

Lastly, you have to handle a man with skill. I am finished when I say this. Sisters, you cannot treat a real man any kind of way. You see, a woman defines her man. She makes him what he is. This means that if you give a woman an ordinary guy, if she has some skill she can produce an extraordinary man. Most women like ready made men. But, the truth is that there is no such thing. Adam needed Eve just like Barack needs Michelle. Why? One always defines the other. Skill says you know when to push him and when to pray for him. Skill says you know when to get him told and when to be quiet and loving. Skill says you know how to lead him with your influence while he stands in his position. Skill says you know how to love him from a distance and touch him when you're up close. Skill! It is what many sisters lack. This woman in the passage had it. How do we know this? It is because her husband was known in the gates of the city. It wasn't because he was so good. It was because she was so great!

In closing, with God on your side you never, ever have to worry about trying to find a good man. God will send the man that He wants you to have when He is ready for you to have him. Until then, don't stand on any corner trying to catch a bus. Buses are temporary means of transportation and what you are looking for is something permanent! When God gets through with you, He will not send you a bus but a private car that is fully loaded and ready for the road ahead!

Chapter 6

I'm A Fool for Learning Some Good Habits from Some Bad Women

"For Women Only"

Some people hate them, while others despise them, many people discuss them, religious women often ridicule them, and still other sisters seek to duplicate them. They have ruined more marriages than the law allows, and they have wrecked more relationships than I have room to mention in this book. Their dress attire is not just sexy it is seductive. Their tattoos are enticing, and their walk is like watching poetry in motion. Their intentions are dangerous, their motives are often hidden, and their appearance is often seen as purely innocent. Their morals are loose, their values are lacking, their habits are not always holy and yet they have their place on the canvas of the pages of Holy Writ. Who are they, you ask? They are bad women!

A good woman can spot her a mile away, older men are often taken swiftly by her mischief, young men get caught up in what she presents, and our culture makes millions on her body and her beauty. Who are they? They are bad women! Make no mistake; every woman is not a good woman. Some women are bad. And, the problem is that there are good men that have good women, but instead of being faithful to the good woman that they have they sometimes fall like fools for the bad woman that means them no good at all. But, why is this? Why do some good men fall for bad women?

Before you leap into this thought-provoking dialogue with your personal views and humble opinions, let's look to the scripture for the answers that God would want us to have. You see, there is a good man in the Bible that falls for a bad woman. Here's what the scripture says, *"And it came to pass afterward, that he loved a woman in the valley of Sorek, whose name was Delilah. And the lords of the Philistines came up unto her, and said unto her, Entice him, and see wherein his great strength lieth, and by what means we may prevail against him, that we may bind him to afflict him: and we will give thee every one of us eleven hundred pieces of silver. And Delilah said to Samson, Tell me, I pray thee, wherein thy great strength lieth, and wherewith thou mightest be bound to afflict thee. And Samson said unto her, If they bind me with seven green withs that were never dried, then shall I be weak, and be as another man. Then the lords of the Philistines brought up to her seven green withs which had not been dried, and she bound him with them"* *(Judges 16:4-8, KJV).* Though Delilah meant Samson absolutely no good at all he still fell face flat for her even though she was a bad woman. And, it is my belief that the same reason why he fell for his bad woman is the exact same reason why men fall for bad women today. So what makes a good man fall for a bad woman?

First of all, she knows how to handle him. This may seem harsh, but it is true nonetheless. Most good women need courses on "man handling." Get this, if a man is a real man (and he is not gay, weak, or sorry) you cannot handle him just any kind of way. Here's a secret that all good women can learn from bad ones. Always handle a man like he's a man. God gave men position and He gave women influence. Use your influence to get what you want from him and let him keep his position. In short, give him what all men must have: R-E-S-P-E-C-T and when you give him what he needs you will always get what you want. If you don't think that this works, look at Delilah, she was a bad woman that got what she wanted from Samson by simply handling him like a man.

Secondly, she knows how to talk to him. Now this is going to get me into trouble, but at the risk of being honest, truthful, godly and helpful I am going to say it. If a man is a real man (and he is not lazy, stupid and shallow) you cannot talk to him just any kind of a way. Bad women know how to talk to a man. Here's a huge secret that all good sisters need to know: screaming and yelling makes him change stations and switch satellites. But, if you know how to say "Baby....listen....I need something from you...." You will get what you need when you need it most. I know, we have been taught that divas put their hands on their hips, roll their necks and get a brother told, right? But, that's why most divas don't have a decent dude. Please get this and hold on to it forever. If you know how to talk to a man you can have it all! You can have his mind, his body, his soul, his money, his heart and his resources. If you can't talk to him right, there is a bad woman that can and will.

Thirdly, she knows how to use her femininity to her advantage. Since I am already in hot water, I may as well say one more thing before this chapter is concluded. If a man is a real man (and he is not on the down low, not foggy in his sexuality and stable in his God-given manhood) he loves every facet of a real woman. He loves her hips, her hands, her legs, her chest, her neck, her eyes, and her feet. What am I saying here? I am saying that bad women know how to wear it and present it. All too often good women do what it takes to get a good man. But, once they have him they swap every good habit for a bad one. In short, if it is ashy, grab some lotion. If it is nappy, dread it or perm it. If it is tacky, fix it up. If it is rough, smooth it out. If it doesn't fit, don't wear it. And, if it is not your best feature, camouflage it! Please hear this, in a real man's mind there is no greater creation on the planet other than true womanhood. So be a woman and be a beautiful one!

For every sister reading this book that has a good man, use these principles to keep him right where he is and know that the only way for you to be the queen is for you to crown him king! And, for every sister that is single that wants a good man remember this, you don't have to be a bad woman to get a good man, but there are some good habits that you can learn from bad women that can help you be the best you that you can be. Use these habits and let the Lord do everything else!

Chapter 7

I'm A Fool for
Driving My Woman Up A Wall

<u>"For Men Only"</u>

"Houston we have a problem!" In case you haven't noticed it, we are struggling to produce healthy, vibrant, long-lasting relationships. In many instances we see love as a "game" to be played rather than a lifetime of commitment to give. The end result of all of this playing has left us with a disproportionate number of single parent households and scores of children born out of wedlock.

Here is the problem. We can attract them, but when things get tough we often find a good reason to detach ourselves from them. We can catch them, but we can't keep them. We can date them, but when the first storm cloud rises we look for reasons to dump them. And, we can talk them into bed for a brief interlude of intimacy, but we are failing at keeping her happy in a relationship that offers any degree of permanency. The reason for this relational mayhem is due to the fact that we refuse to take our relational instructions from the Lord. God has a great deal to say about how we treat women. Obey Him, and you will not only make a sister smile, you will not just make her happy, and you will not just make her scream, but you will literally drive her up a wall!

Here's what the Bible says, ***Thy wife shall be as a fruitful vine by the sides of thine house: thy children like olive plants round about thy table" (Psalms 128:3, KJV)***. It is a beautiful metaphor used to etymologically paint pictures with words on the frontal lobe of the intellect. David says when a real man loves a woman right she will be just like a fruit bearing plant that's climbing along the wall of his house. Now if that's what you want in your relationship, here's what you need to do to get it.

First of all, you have to put a ring on her finger and place her in a nice house. Here's the real truth about any godly relationship; shacking up is out and marriage is in. The sister in the passage is described as a "wife." For the sake of socio-cultural clarity, she is a woman with a man that has made a covenant with God to remain with her until death comes to receive one of them to be with the Lord. And, the passage says that she is in a house. Now for the benefit for every brother reading this missive, you are not required to buy her a mansion. Your house can be a sweet little sugar-shack. However, it is your responsibility to put a roof over her head. And for every sister that is reading this chapter even though it is labeled for men only and has moved a broke, weak man into their house knowing that the man that they are with does not have any place to call a home but his mother's house, here's a word of advice, run! You are in for trouble and you don't know it! Brothers, a man must be able to provide a roof to cover his head before he deserves a woman in his bed under his roof. This may seem tight, but I promise you that it is right. Remember, a ring and a house will drive her up a wall.

Secondly, you must hold her tenderly and treat her like a flower. After you put a ring on her finger and place her in a house, you must learn to treat her like a treasure. This means you can't treat her just any kind of way. Believe it or not, this is a two-way street. Sisters, if you want to be treated like a queen, you have to handle him like he's a king. And men, if you want her to talk to you like a queen, you have to handle her like she's a fruitful vine. This is the metaphor given in the Bible. Your woman is a fruitful vine. If you want fruit from a fruitful vine, you have to water it, take care of it, and treat it with tender love and care. You can't treat it like trash and then return and think that you can get some fruit. Remember, if you don't treat her with tender love and care, you can't have any fruit.No fruit juice, no fruit cocktail, no warm fruit pie fresh from the oven, and no steaming hot fruit cobbler. In fact, if you fail to treat her well she will go on a fruit strike and place the garden on lock down. But, if you know how to water her, love her, listen to her, talk to her and care for her you will get fruit in return. In fact, you will have so much fruit that you will have fruit preserves. The Bible says that your fruit will start growing up the side of your house. In short, you will drive her up a wall.

Thirdly, you need to help her with the kids and the things around the house. To provide for her is one thing, but for you to assist her with those provisions is another. Help with the kids and the house. In the passage it says that a man's children will be like olive plants around his table. This is a wonderful picture of healthy, productive kids that have the parental love and touch of both parents in the home. In our culture a man that helps with the home is seen as feminine and weak, but I submit to you that the Bible shows us that such a man is masculine and strong! Help with the house. Help with the kids. It will bless you in the long run. In fact, here's a secret that every brother should hold near and dear to his heart. If you touch what she touches while she is in the house, she will touch you with love and passion when you get home. Make up the bed, wash some clothes, do the dishes, go to the grocery store with her list and do the shopping, help her. When you get through doing this, it will drive her up a wall.

And lastly, you need to help her as she grows and produces. We live in an age of productive, career-minded women. Some men feel threatened by this type of productivity. A real man is not afraid of this. Just because she produces, it does not make her the leader of your home. Keep in mind, God gave men position and He gave women influence. No matter what she produces, you are the leader so thank God for what she does and encourage her along the way. In fact, grab a set of pom-poms and become her greatest cheerleader and supporter. After all, what she produces is for your team because she is wearing your jersey. When you support her dreams, ambitions, and career choices it will drive her completely up a wall.

Chapter 8

I'm A Fool for Being A Real Man That's Rough Around the Edges

"For Men Only"

There are numerous definitions for a person that lives under the banner and auspices of one who is a "thug." Webster says that a thug is "a vicious, cruel ruffian, murderer and robber." Historically a group within India claims to have been the first thugs on the planet. In 1810, when the British colonized India, there was a group of defiant men that resisted against social change. They were known for snuffing out British leaders and killing them by way of strangulation. These men who stood against the British regime were called "thugs" or "thugee" for their thuggish ways. However, the late rapper Tupac Shakur said that a thug was "someone who is going through struggles, has gone through struggles, and continues somehow to live day by day with nothing from them. That person is a thug. A thug is not a gangster, a thug is a person just trying to survive in the game of life." And most people that have been raised and reared in the midst of urban blight and economic decay know a thug to be a person that will do what they have to do, so that they can do what they need to do. All in all, a thug is not a nice title to put on anyone.

Thanks to the post-modern hip-hop subculture, when we say "thug" today the persona and imago dei is that of a man that you would not want to meet on a dimly lit street corner at sundown. His morals are poor, his record is tarnished, his ethics are shady, his hands will fight, and his earnings are always questionable. His children are scattered around town like sesame seeds on a hamburger bun. His language is foul; his attitude is always subject to change (sweet sometimes and crazy the next). His habits are bad, his virtues are limited, his educational portfolio is brief, his hustle is on, his testimony is real, and his women are plenteous. Now, knowing all of that, why is it that a thug never has a hard time finding a woman? Wait before you bash the sisters by calling them desperate, good for nothing and hard up I contend that there is something in a thug that makes a real woman love him, and it's biblical!

When you look at the kind of men that God used, they were all men with some rough edges. In our culture we would call some of them thugs. Solomon was a great King but he had a hustlers mentality, way too many women and a hit man whose name was Benaiah; King David (Solomon's Father) was a great musician, but could squabble with the best of them and drop a giant with a blow to head; Noah had a drinking habit that at times could go out of control; Peter, one of the Lord's inner circle of disciples carried a knife with him and would use it at any time, and Moses would kill you if he had to. Here's what the Bible says, *"And it came to pass in those days, when Moses was grown, that he went out unto his brethren, and looked on their burdens: and he spied an Egyptian smiting an Hebrew, one of his brethren. And he looked this way and that way, and when he saw that there was no man, he slew the Egyptian, and hid him in the sand" (Exodus 2:11-12, KJV).* Still with the hands of a murderer, Moses landed one of the most beautiful women of his era whose name was Zipporah. What did Moses have that attracted this woman to him even though he had a questionable background? Get this; what she found in him is the same thing that make women today love a thug. So what did she find? Let's briefly explore these findings as we embrace the fact that all real men that are both saved and celibate will have some rough edges. Not only do real men have some rough edges but women are attracted to men that have them. So why do some women love a thug?

They love them because they are certain about their masculinity. Here's the truth, and it may be considered sexist and wrong, but real women do not want a soft, sorry, weak, spineless man. Sisters want a real man that is sure about who he is in his manhood. Moses was without a doubt a great man. He was not afraid to stand alone, he was strong enough to lead, he was bold enough to confront Pharaoh and smooth enough to sweep Zipporah off of her feet. He was a man. We live in an era right now when some men are not really men. And someone has put out a bad rumor that women want men like this. But, nothing could be further from the truth. Women find it attractive when a man is a man. The only women who don't find this attractive are those who don't really want a man to begin with.

You will never ever meet a thug that struggles with his sexuality. He is always 100% man and real women love, like and value that part of his character.

They love them because they always provide a sense of safety and security. Okay, let's go ahead and say it so that we can clear the air. A thug is not the kind of man that a sister should marry. But, one of his vices is actually a God-given virtue. He will fight! A thug will lay hands on you and he is not praying with oil. He will put some bruises on you that soap will not wash away. And, because of this harsh nature, he possesses the fortitude to provide a climate for those that he loves that says "you are going to be alright because you are with me." Moses never had a problem protecting all of Israel, and that included his woman. Likewise, a real woman is attracted to a man that makes her feel safe and secure. No real sister wants a man that runs from the dark, hides because he is afraid and weeps because he is weak. Security by way of masculinity is always attractive.

Women love thugs because they are always deeply rooted in loyalty. Thugs are always the "ride or die" type of men. This is a cultural colloquialism that means that once you are in you are in and there is no getting out. This means that no matter what happens, we are in it to win it together. Believe it or not, all real women love men that are committed to something. Years ago there was a common cliché that said that women loved a man in a uniform. Why? Because, in order to wear a uniform, he had to be committed to the armed forces. Without a doubt, Moses is loyal to God and is willing to continue alone if he has to do it by himself. In my view, this made his wife say, "now that's a real man."

In closing, every real man has a little thug in him. It is apart of his manhood that God put there that cannot ever be moved. It is this part of a man's nature that God puts under control when he is saved that brings him into humility and meekness. These admirable qualities mentioned above are some that all real men need to keep and use each day. There's nothing wrong with a man who has some rough edges, as long as he is in the hands of God and the Lord is doing all of the trim work on his life. Real women love real men and this will never ever change!

Chapter 9

I'm A Fool for Keeping
My Ex's In the Right Place

There are twenty-six letters in the English alphabetical system that includesthe five vowels, A, E, I, O, U and twenty-one consonants. The use of these alphabets shape a system of words so vast, until there is no single answer to the number of words and word phrases that can be constructed in the English language using them. Yet, there is one alphabet that when used can speak volumes all on its own. It is the letter "X". Uses of "X" range from the largely contemporary to the simple and from the complex to the mundane. For instance, if you like comic books and movies you might like the "X-Men" and if you like to play video games you might like the "X-Box." If you are from the old school, then the game of "tic-tac-toe" is your thing where you can find "X's" and "O's" fighting on a clean sheet of paper. If you are in grade school and you took a spelling test and failed to get a perfect score you will find at least one big red "X" on your paper. Football commentators and coaches often use "X's" and "O's" to represent the offensive and defensive players on the field when written on a chalkboard, and a great game show on TV right now is called the "X-Factor".

While on the subject of "X-Factors" it brings us to the universal language of mathematics and arithmetic whereby "X" represents an unknown integer. For example, $2X + 3 = 19$ is a linear equation where $X = 8$ (I did this all by myself, can you believe it?). The letter "X" has even been used by frustrated African Americans of the Nation of Islam for years that recognize and object to the tyranny caused by the European slave trade. In this regard, some people of color have replaced their surname with the letter "X" as did El Hajj Melik El Shabazz whom we know to be Malcolm X. But, the most popular use of the alphabet "X" means to delete, to erase, to get rid of or to do away with. To blot out.

Interestingly, "EX" as a prefix according to most linguists that means "without the former with regard to the future." It means to take away. With this in mind, I believe that every real Christian should have a "used to be story." If you do not have a "used to be story " that means that you are still being what you used to be! In short, you may not be perfect, but knowing Jesus should have made a change in your life by now. That change means that you are an "ex" something. Therefore, if you are saved and you were a liar before you met Jesus then today you should be an ex-liar. If you were steeped in fornication before you met God then today you should be an ex-fornicator. If you were an alcoholic before you met Jesus Christ then today you should be an ex-alcoholic. If you could scoop up somebody's husband before you got married and have them wrapped up in adultery before the Lord got a hold of you, certainly by now you should be ex-adulterer. If you have a boyfriend that really dogged you then surely you would not want to continue tolerating that foolishness and that would make him your ex-boyfriend. If you messed around and married that joker he may now even be your ex-husband. And, for the sake of inclusiveness, if you are a brother that had a crazy sister, she might be your ex-girlfriend and if you married that live wire she may now be your ex-wife.

Now here's our problem, in many instances the reason why we can't seem to move forward is because our "Ex's" need some "X's"! There are times when what is behind us hinders us from getting what is ahead of us. When that happens, you need to issue out some more "X's". There are some things that you need to get rid of. That great Apostle from Tarsus puts it on this order as he writes the church in Philippi, *"Not as though I had already attained, either were already perfect: but I follow after, if that I may apprehend that for which also I am apprehended of Christ Jesus. Brethren, I count not myself to have apprehended: but this one thing I do, forgetting those things which are behind, and reaching forth unto those things which are before, I press toward the mark for the prize of the high calling of God in Christ Jesus" (Phil. 3:12-14).* You see, Paul needed some "X's" and so do you.

There are people reading this message that are haunted by old habits. Today is the day for you to give your "EX" an "X". That stuff behind you is what you used to be. There are those of you who struggle with forgiveness and you keep the pain of your past alive because you will not let it go. Today you're going to give your "EX" and "X." There are those of you who have people from your past that just walk in and out of your life over, and over, and over and over again. You need an "X" for your "EX". Some of you have seen the same demons just resurface all of your life. But, this is a message of liberation tucked away in this chapter. What you need; what you must have; and what is required of you is to have an "X" for all of your "EX's". But, how can we make sure that our "EX's" get permanent "X's" so that we can continue moving forward with Jesus Christ?

You must remember that you are just as imperfect as the rest. Get this, none of us have arrived and one sure sign that we have not arrived is the fact that all of us have imperfections that surface as weaknesses when it comes to some of our ex's. You may not be weak for everything but you are weak for something. It may not be a rum and coke, but those dice get you every time. It may not be short and thick it just might be tall, slender and cute. It might not be the one with the dreadlocks; it could be the one with the bald head. It might not be him over there but this one over here. It is human imperfection at its best and Paul admits to it. He says "Not as though I had already attained, neither were already perfect...." In other words, I do not have it all together yet and therefore, I need some more "X's" and some new "Ex's!" Here's a good question for you to consider. What are some imperfections, habits and happenings that you need to give an "X" to? Here's a Word from the Lord; give those things an "X" that need them so that you can create some new "EX's."

Secondly, you must recognize that it is imperative for you to get past your "EX" so that you get what is next. One of the biggest reasons that you really want to give your "EX" an "X" is because your "EX" can keep you from getting what's next. You see, your "EX" is behind you and what is next is ahead of you and you cannot go both directions at the same time. But our problem is that our "EX" is not an "EX" yet so it keeps us from getting what the Lord says is next! Paul tells us how to handle it right. In the text he says, "...forgetting those things which are behind and reaching (stretching) forth unto those things which are before..." Forgetting is the Greek word epee-lan-than-omai. It means to leave in the dust. It is in the present tense and passive voice. Therefore, it is something that happens in the past with affects on the future and it is something that you must do for yourself. God is always in the business of getting us to what is next. For some it is the next job, the next relationship, the next assignment, the next level and even the next dimension. Don't miss what is next for your life fooling around with an "EX!" Move forward in the faith knowing that the best is still yet to come.

Lastly, you must realize that what is next is good, but your destiny is not found in what is next but in what is best. People often get excited about what's next, but you ain't shouted until you've seen what is best! If you could see the plans that God has for your life you would give your "EX's" and "X" so fast it would make your head spin. When God wanted to bless you He did not send you just anything or anybody. He gave you His best. Jesus Christ died for you, so that you could live for Him and not just have what's next, but have what is best. One word of caution about what is best, and that is, you will never ever get what is best without having to press. Here's what the text says, "I press towards the mark for the prize of the high calling of God in Christ Jesus." Okay, here it is there is a press and there is a prize. People often want the prize but they do not want the press. We want the muscle, but we don't want the gym. We want financial stability but we don't want to budget. We want a husband but we don't want to give up fornication. We want a wife but we don't want to stop cheating. And, we want to be made high but we do not want to humble ourselves and go low. The word press is dee-oko and it means to play hurt. Here's the shout of the day: what's best always comes with a bruise and the prize always comes with a price! But, if you are willing to run on and sacrifice it all for the sake of Jesus Christ, your "EX's" will get "X's" and you will get what is best every time.

Chapter 10

I'm A Fool for
Good Bye's and Benedictions

Not long ago, while sitting in an airport in Jacksonville, Florida, I noticed something that really caught my attention. I saw people saying goodbye and the tears that came along with it. Let's be honest for a moment, goodbye's can be difficult. When the coffin closes on a loved one that is gone, but never forgotten, goodbye can bring tears to your eyes. When a child goes off to college or when your little one goes to school on the first day it can make you cry. It is during moments like this that goodbye can be difficult. But all goodbyes are not tearjerkers. In fact, there are times when goodbye can bless you like crazy.

The tragedy of human relationships is not seen in the people that hurt us, neither is it seen in the people that use us or violate our trust, but it is seen in the people that we hold onto for far too long. In this regard, there is a blessing in saying goodbye. When you have given someone your love, time, commitment, and money and they don't have enough sense to appreciate it, if they leave, then let them go. Wave goodbye and never look back. If you are dating someone and they are cheating on you right now, bless yourself and say goodbye before you need a divorce decree later on. Let them walk because they are blocking your blessings and wasting your time. If you are giving your job your all, and I mean if you are giving it one hundred percent and then some, and your employer does not find your contributions valuable, your time important, and your partnership a necessity, then bless yourself and move to greater ground. Hear this and hold on to it, there is a blessing in cutting people off, letting them go, giving them the benediction, waving from a distance and saying goodbye!

Here's what the Bible says. ***"They left us, but they were not part of us. For if they had been part of us, they would have stayed with us. They simply made it clear that none of them was really part of us" (1 John 2:19, NIV)***. Can you hear God speaking to you yet? Here's what God is saying, and it is wonderful news for many of you reading this book that struggle with holding on too long. If you have tried to help them, love them, bless them, invest in them, lift them up, and pray for them, when they leave, let them go. When they stop calling you, put your phone down. When they depart from your presence bless yourself and say goodbye! But, how can saying goodbye be a blessing for you?

First of all, if they left you, they left because they wanted to leave and you burden yourself by begging them to stay. Get this and never forget it: you cannot make people love you back! You cannot make people feel about you like you feel about them. People vote with their feet. So when they walk, give them the freedom to do it. Here's what the passage says, "They left us..." In other words, it was an act of human volition. It was a decision that they made. It's so deep, people often make a decision to walk into your life and when you let them in they get what they came for and leave. In the vocation of psychology we call that narcissistic use. It happens when people use you to accommodate their own desires at your expense. In short, only sick people do this. When people use you pray for them like you would anybody else that was ill because they are sick. Remember, when a person leaves you because they wanted to, you should want them to! Bless yourself, rejoice and say goodbye.

Secondly, if they left you, their part in your life's destiny is over. It is okay to hit replay on a CD or DVD player, iPod or mp3 player if that was your favorite song. But, it can be horrific to hit replay when it comes to people, especially when their part in your life is over. John says it like this, "...they were not apart of us..." In other words, their part is over because they have taught us the lessons that they were in our lives to teach. Here's a good question for you to think on; what lessons did you learn from them? Did you learn the lesson that says, "Everyone that says 'I love you' really doesn't mean it?" Did you learn the lesson that says, "Some of the people that say 'I will always be here for you' are lying?" And, did you learn the one that says, "When people tell you they've got your back they can sometimes be the one's with a knife in their hands?" Like an actor on a stage when people leave, look at it as if to say, "Their part in the grand production of my life is over." Thank God for the lessons that they taught you and say goodbye.

Lastly, if they do not leave the promise will not come. Two blessings cannot stand in the same pair of shoes. If you hold onto your past, your future will never arrive! You see the Bible says, "...they made it clear that they were not a part of us." In other words, they were not apart of the promise. Now the shouting news about this lesson is that if the promise has not come, it is yet on the way. Are you rejoicing yet? You should be if you have people that have left you. If the people that left your life were not a part of the promise, it means that what's behind you is what has been and what's in front of you is the blessing of what is still yet to come. This is why you bless yourself when you say goodbye to people that leave because there are others coming that are not there yet that will be providentially placed by God just to bless you!

This chapter is for people that love too hard, give too much, and hold on too long. This is for people that have wept over people that have used them, lost sleep over people that did not want them and tried to get people to love them when they did not want to. Say this like you mean it, declare this like it will heal you from the inside out, and pray this in your spirit like you want to bless yourself, "Goodbye, Goodbye, Goodbye, Goodbye, Goodbye to everyone, anyone, and everybody that has ever walked out of my life!"

Chapter 11

I'm a Fool for Saying No,
When My Flesh is Saying Yes

It is going to happen to you, if it hasn't happened already. You are going to meet somebody that will make your flesh scream, "Yes!" In most instances, you know it right off the bat. As soon as you see them, your mind's eye repeats the mantra found in fairytale books around the world, "Lookie, Lookie, I see a cookie" and your stomach is growling, your body is on fire, and your hormones are out of control. If it is not something that happens at first sight; it can sneak up on you like a black hawk helicopter that comes in under the radar of your moral regard. You may have known the person for quite a while and all you have been is just friends. One conversation leads to laughter, laughter can lead to a talk and lunch; laughter, a talk and lunch can lead to just sitting on the couch; but laughter, a talk, and lunch coupled with just sitting on the couch snuggled up leads to "somebody call the fire department, my flesh is on fire!"

Make no mistake; this earth suit that we are in is not to be played with. Never, ever trust the flesh. It will mislead you every time. Your flesh will make you lie to yourself and say things like "I am not going to have sex with this person." "All we are doing is just relaxing together." And, what about this one, "I can stop when I want to, so I am not going all of the way" and before you know it, you look up and you have to ask yourself the question, "what happened to my clothes?" There is an old cliché that says, "don't play with fire or you will get burned." Here's an even better one for every single saint that dares to be celibate in a world of promiscuity, "don't gamble with your flesh because you will lose that bet every single time."

Saying no to your flesh is not always easy. When you want to be held, saying no is not easy. When you want to be kissed, touched, caressed, and physically loved, saying no is not like passing up the dessert tray after a huge meal. It is more like saying no to a buffet after you have not eaten for three or four days. You need that food, your mouth can taste it, your flesh says go for it (God will understand), but your Lord is saying, "that's the wrong table, it doesn't belong to you, put that down!"

A lifestyle of celibacy is one that will only come to those that have made decisions to let God meet their needs. This is what makes fornication and masturbation wrong. Both of them are your attempt to meet your own needs while God is waiting to do that for you. Your flesh is dangerous when it comes to matters of sexual intimacy. If you plan to say no when your flesh is saying yes you must learn to do what Joseph did when he was confronted with Potiphar's wife. Here's how the story flows," *And it came to pass after these things, that his master's wife cast her eyes upon Joseph; and she said, lie with me. But he refused, and said unto his master's wife, behold, my master wotteth not what is with me in the house, and he hath committed all that he hath to my hand; there is none greater in this house than I; neither hath he kept back anything from me but thee, because thou art his wife: how then can I do this great wickedness, and sin against God? And it came to pass, as she spake to Joseph day by day, that he hearkened not unto her, to lie by her, or to be with her. And it came to pass about this time, that Joseph went into the house to do his business; and there was none of the men of the house there within. And she caught him by his garment, saying, lie with me: and he left his garment in her hand, and fled, and got him out"* (Gen. 39:7-12, KJV).

This narrative is like a scene from a reality television show. This sister who is married has been exposed to this handsome man who is working in her house while her husband is gone and her flesh is on fire. His abs is tight, his chest is muscular, his arms are strong, his chin is square and his eyes are light brown. He is good looking. Potiphar's wife is not bad looking herself. She is an Egyptian Queen. Her hips are full, her stomach is flat, her lips are kissable and she is in her house lounging around. Can you see this picture in your mind? Joseph is looking at this woman like you would look a cool bottle of water on a hot day, but he will not do it. He could pick her up, lay her out and travel to sin city, but he will not do it. He is able to say no to his flesh. Now here is the great news of the day for every single person that is seeking to be celibate; if Joseph can do it, you can do it. The question is how do you say no, when your flesh is saying yes?

First of all, you must refuse to sell your master short. I may not know you at all, but I do that know God has been good to you. He has forgiven you for the mistakes of your past, He has favored your life with merciful love, He has kept you all of your life and you have seen Him increase you in so many ways that it is enough to bring tears to your eyes. For you to fall to your flesh in the sin of fornication is to sell God short. Hear these words and let them rest in your heart and soul: don't sell out! Look at the life of Joseph. His family has turned against him, but God has been good to him; his brothers wanted to have him killed, but the Lord has spared him and he has faced death in a foreign land, but the Lord has shown him the kind of favor that he would take what was meant for his bad, and turn it around and use it for his good. When Joseph considers what his Master has done for him, he does not have sex with Mrs. Potiphar because in order to sex her he has to sell out on God and he refused to do that. It is worthy of mention that nowhere in the verse does it say that Joseph didn't want to do it. He wanted to do it, but he chose not to.

Secondly, you must resist the advances of the flesh that take you the wrong direction. Listen, you know you are headed in the wrong direction when you can see a clear trend of activity that pulls you away from your walk with God. The enemy uses your flesh to pull you away from the Lord just like a child is pulled away chasing a ball that dribbles out of the safety of the front yard into the street where there is oncoming traffic. This is why you have to be careful with simple advances because one of them feeds the other. In verse 10 of the story the Bible says that Mrs. Potiphar bothered Joseph "...day by day..." She knew what time Joseph was supposed to be at work and what part of the house he was supposed to be working in and she made it her business to be right there with her advances. Bear in mind, the only way to deal effectively with advances is with counter attacks that will keep your flesh in check, your mind on God and your seducer at bay. When they say, "do you want some company?" You say, "Thanks for the offer, but I am good." When they say "let me help you with that" You should say, "You're very kind but, I've got it." And when they brush up against you in a way that you know is not the norm, you say, "Excuse me, but I really didn't appreciate that." Remember, advances lead to avalanches if they are accepted and not rejected. Never accept fleshly advances. They will take you in the wrong direction.

Lastly you must remember that the testing of your flesh comes before the blessing of your future. Please keep this in mind: it is not the heat of the moment that is so important it is your moral integrity that matters the most. Believe it or not, your future depends on how you function when no one can see you. Faith that is not tested should never be trusted and will never, ever be rewarded. There are those of you who have struggled here time and time again. Every time you think you are really committed, someone else shows up in your life and they pull you away from your walk with God, using the desires of your flesh as bait. But, when it is all finished you have failed again. To you I say that the reason why you keep taking the same test over and over is because you keep failing it time and time again. Joseph passed his test and he is promoted in Egypt to the second highest man in the country. Did you get that? He was tested with a woman in the dark, but was promoted to lead the nation in the light. Joseph understood the real secret of Christian celibacy. Here it is and hold it forever: if you run from the flesh you will run right into God's favor! God has great plans for your future; in fact, the desires of your heart await you. But, you must prove yourself worthy by saying no to the flesh and yes to the Lord.

Chapter 12

I'm A Fool for God Because
I Know He Really Loves Me

Not long ago I overheard a conversation that took place between two young ladies at church. They are both Christians and very attractive. Of course, they were not talking to me, but I took the time to eavesdrop and just be downright nosy. After listening to the conversation for a moment I concluded that they were both single and wanted to be married. Why was I able to deduce this from just listening to them? Both of them talked about how lonely they were. Like the desert has no water, they had no men or even dates in the distance. Here's a side note: isn't it interesting, when you are seeing someone everyone wants to give you a shout or show you some interest. But, when you are single and alone, you're really all by yourself. I don't know why it's like that, but it's just the way that it is.

Back to the story. The young women are talking and the discussion is on how real love is so hard to find and how lonely they are and how things are just barren. While they are in discussion with each other, one of the young ladies who serves as a ministry leader hears them and rushes over to them like a school bus pulling into a schoolyard to pick up kids without the red lights flashings to tell oncoming traffic to halt. She said to them "Girl, I used to be like you guys are right now until about four years ago. I am so much better right now." One of the lonely cute girls said, "You are way too spiritual for us. We are just keeping it real." But, the ministry leader dropped something on them that blessed me and empowered them. She said, "how would you feel if you were with each other all day long, but at the end of the day told everyone how lonely you were?" Of course the lonely young ladies said that they would feel horrible. That's when the young ministry leader said, "that's how God feels when you say you're lonely and He's been waiting on some of your attention all day!" All I could say was, "Wow!"

God loves you so very much. He has been there with you from the very beginning. In fact, before you were conceived God had you in His plans

Dr. John R. Adolph

and He loves you. He has plans to bless you; He loves you enough to die to prove His love for you; and, He longs for a deeper, more meaningful relationship with you. He wants the kind of relationship with you where the two of you can become friends. He wants you to know that He has your back and He wants you to have His. Picture this in your mind. He watches you sleep, He touches you to wake you each morning, He watches you as you rise, and He pays close attention to you all day long. When you get dressed, He's there. As you drive to work, He's there. As you labor on your job, He's there and as you discuss how lonely you are from time to time, He is there. His face is saddened because no matter how much He loves you and provides for you, He can't get you to fall in love with Him. He's tried everything. He's tried loving, giving, forgiving, blessing, and protecting you. He's tried favor, material goods, increase, overflow, and even healing, but nothing works. Even though He is there for you somehow you still end up lonely just like the two young ladies in the church foyer.

Be honest about it. Have you ever been there? If you have, the conclusion of this book is going to empower you. Instead of looking for love and companionship in people, I want to challenge you to seek that same thing in Jesus Christ. This is the real key to celibacy. Intimacy with God is like nothing that you have ever experienced before in your life! With this in mind, you are going to plan a date to share intimately with your special someone, but your special one this time will be God. Now in order for a date to really be good, you must have several components present to pull it off right, so do the same with the Lord:

1. Start by telling the Lord that you are planning a special date with Him. Tell Him that you really want to be with Him. I mean, after all that He's done for you, He's done things that no one else has ever done.

2. Pick a place and time for the meeting. You can use a hotel room or a nice, quiet place in your house. Just make sure that you are all alone. No cell phone. No iPad. No outside interference.

3. Chose a nice outfit. You don't want to meet your new date wearing just any old thing.

4. Pick some great music. Ambiance can be everything. If you need to light a candle or two so that you can set the mood.

5. Write Him a card and tell Him how much you love Him and desire a relationship with Him. Tell him how much you need Him and apologize for looking past Him in loneliness to people when He had been standing there the whole time.

6. Sing Him a song. Okay, this may seem silly, especially for those that cannot sing at all. But trust me, singing before God is an act of worship that will make Him shower you with His presence.

7. Plan a nice dinner with Him. Prepare a meal for yourself or order room service. But, receive it with joy and tell God thank you for having dinner with you.

8. After dinner get a good Bible and read the Gospel of John. It will bless you!

9. Take a nice long bath and while you bathe ask Him to cleanse you again from past sins and mistakes. Play some wonderful worship music and tell God thank you for health, strength, and physical blessing. Pray and talk with Him and do not be shocked at all if you weep, cry, and worship. Trust me, it is going to happen.

10. Get into bed and tell God that you want Him to hold you.

11. If you've not been really trying to practice a life of celibacy, admit to God that you have been doing relationships wrong and that you want to do them His way from now on, but that you're going to need His help.

12. Fall asleep in the arms of the Lord only to rise the next morning with a renewed commitment to live for Him, never to be lonely in His presence again, because He has always loved you and has been waiting on you to love Him back.

Celibacy may not make sense according to the world's standards. But when you fall in love with Jesus Christ, it will make all of the sense in the world. Sex and seduction are all around us, but you have a Savior who dwells within you and loves you like crazy. He is madly in love with you and wants you to love Him back. There will always be people who think that you have lost your mind when you decide to live a celibate lifestyle, but remember, it is always worth it. Celibacy is for fools.